Independent Schools
Examinations Board

# RELIGIOUS STUDIES
## ISEB Revision Guide

# Michael Wilcockson

Independent Schools
Examinations Board

**www.galorepark.co.uk**

GALORE PARK

Published by ISEB Publications, an imprint of Galore Park Publications Ltd
19/21 Sayers Lane, Tenterden, Kent TN30 6BW
www.galorepark.co.uk

Design and typesetting Typetechnique

Illustrations by Gwyneth Williamson and Simon Tegg

Printed by Replika Press, India

ISBN-13: 978 0 903627 62 7

First published April 2008, reprinted May 2008, September 2008

Details of other ISEB Revision Guides for Common Entrance, examination
papers and Galore Park publications are available at www.galorepark.co.uk

Front cover photo: Damir Sagolj/Reuters/Corbis UK Ltd.

# About the author

Michael Wilcockson was brought up in Cambridge and studied Theology at Balliol College, Oxford. After completing his PGCE at Pembroke College, Cambridge he was appointed Head of Divinity at Aldenham School and later at The Leys School, Cambridge. From 1996 he has been Head of Divinity at Eton College. He was a Farmington Fellow at Harries Manchester College, Oxford in 2003. He is a Chief Examiner for A Level Religious Studies for a large examination board and chief setter for Common Entrance Religious Studies for ISEB, as well as an author of many textbooks. He has recently been made a Fellow of the Institute of Educational Assessors.

# Acknowledgements

I would like to thank the following people: Emma Wilcockson, Oliver Bullock, Alison Wilcockson and Nicholas Oulton.

# Contents

WhoWas
Jesus →

# Introduction

This Revision guide covers Syllabus A of the Common Entrance Religious Studies examination. The chapters are set out to correspond to the layout of the examination paper. Chapter 1 lists out the key words and ideas that may be tested in Sections 1 and 2 of the paper.

Chapters 2 and 3 cover the Bible texts which may be tested in Sections 1 and 2 of the examination. They begin with Part a – short definition question; Part b – a summary of the Bible story; Part c – an interpretation of the Bible story and its ideas; Part d – evaluation and contemporary ideas, for each of the Bible stories. Sample questions are given for each section and there is a Test Yourself section at the end of each chapter. You can use the Test Yourself answers at the back of the book to help you structure your answers.

Chapters 4–9 cover the World Religions section of the examination paper and is a summary of the main ideas of each religion, with a Test Yourself section at the end of each chapter.

Good luck with your revision. Revision is never a very exciting activity but if you do it well it can be quite satisfying and it might even mean you enjoy doing the examination itself! That, with luck, will help you get your place at senior school.

## The syllabus and your exam

If you have *not* submitted coursework you have **60** minutes to complete the examination. For summer 2008 the examination will offer the following choices:

- Choose **one** question from **Section 1** (Old Testament) from a choice of four. Spend no more than **20 minutes** on this question.

- Choose **one** question from **Section 2** (New Testament) from a choice of four. Spend no more than **20 minutes** on this question.

- Choose **four** questions from **Section 3** (World Religions) from a choice of 30. Spend no more than **5 minutes** per question in this section.

If you have submitted coursework then you have **40 minutes** to complete Sections 1 and 2.

From September 2008 the choice of questions will change:

- Choose **one** question from **Section 1** (20 minutes) and **one** question from **Section 2** (20 minutes)

**OR**

- Choose **two** questions from **Section 1** (40 minutes)

**OR**

- Choose **two** questions from **Section 2** (40 minutes)

**AND**

- Choose **four** questions from **Section 3** (5 minutes for each question)

If you have submitted coursework then only complete Sections 1 and/or 2.

## Sections 1 and 2

There are **four** questions in Section 1 and **four** questions from Section 2 and you have to answer **one** question from each Section.

Each question has **four parts** which become increasingly more complex.

- **Part a** briefly tests factual knowledge or asks for a definition of a word or phrase.

- **Part b** tests factual knowledge of a Biblical story.

- **Part c** tests your ability to interpret the story.

- **Part d** tests your ability to discuss and evaluate a contemporary issue raised by the story.

## Section 3

There are **30** questions in Section 3. You have to answer **four** questions. Your teacher will have told you which religion or religions you have studied and therefore which questions you should attempt.

- If you have submitted **coursework** to your senior school then there is no need to revise for this section.

# Tips on revising
## Get the best out of your brain

- Give your brain plenty of oxygen by **exercising**. You can revise more effectively if you feel fit and well.

- **Eat healthy** food while you are revising – your brain works better when you give it good fuel.

- **Think positively**. Give your brain positive messages so that it will want to study.

- **Keep calm**. If your brain is stressed it will not operate effectively.

- Take **regular breaks** during your study time.

- Get enough **sleep**. Your brain will carry on sorting out what you have revised while you sleep.

## Get the most from your revision

- **Don't** work for hours without a break. Revise for 20-30 minutes, then take a five minute break.

- **Do** good things in your breaks: listen to your favourite music, eat healthy food, drink some water, do some exercise or juggle. **Don't** read a book, watch TV or play on the computer as it will conflict with what your brain is trying to learn.

- When you go back to your revision, **review** what you have just learnt.

- Regularly review the facts you have learnt.

## Get motivated

- Set yourself some **goals** and promise yourself a treat when the exams are over.

- Make the most of all the **expertise** and talent available to you at school and at home. If you don't understand something, ask your teacher to explain.

- Get **organised**. Find a quiet place to revise and make sure you have all the equipment you need.

- Use year and weekly **planners** to help you organise your time so that you revise all subjects equally. (Available for download from www.galorepark.co.uk)

- Use topic and subject **checklists** to help you keep on top of what you are revising. (Available for download from www.galorepark.co.uk)

## Know what to expect in the exam

- Use past papers to familiarise yourself with the **format** of the exam.

- Make sure you understand the **language** examiners use.

## Before the exam

- Have all your **equipment** and pens ready the night before.

- Make sure you are at your best by getting a good night's **sleep** before the exam.

- Have a good **breakfast** in the morning.

- Take some **water** into the exam if you are allowed.

- Think **positively** and keep **calm**.

## During the exam

- Have a **watch** or clock on your desk. Work out how much time you need to allocate to each question and try to stick to it.

- Make sure you **read and understand** the instructions and rules on the front of the exam paper.

- Allow some time at the start to read and **consider** the questions carefully before writing anything.

- Read all the questions at least twice. **Don't rush** into answering before you have a chance to think about it.

- If a question is particularly hard move on to the next one. Go back to it if you have time at the end.

- **Check** your answers make sense if you have time at the end.

## Tips for revising Religious Studies

- When using this revision guide, cover up the page and write down as many of the ideas that you can remember, *then* look again at the guide.

- Make sure you refer specifically to words in bold.

- Make sure you first learn all the key words which the examination board prescribe. These can be found in Chapter 1.

- Learn the other words and phrases in Chapter 1 first. These will help you develop your own technical vocabulary and provide you with examples of people and their ideas.

- Use the suggested 'for' and 'against' arguments to begin your own ideas. Make sure you make a note in your own thoughts so you can use these in the examination.

- Practice makes perfect so get your own copy of *Preparing for Common Entrance Religious Studies* (Michael Wilcockson). You could also contact Galore Park and purchase some past papers.

**For more tips on how to get the best from your revision and exams, see *Study Skills* by Elizabeth Holtom, published by Galore Park.**

# How to cope with the exam

- Try to get a good night's sleep the night before the exam. You will be able to approach the exam much more positively if you feel refreshed. Do not eat too late the night before and have a good breakfast in the morning.

- Check that you have everything you need to take into the exam. Take at least two pens in case one runs out. Your teacher will tell you if there are any other items you need to take as well.

- If your school allows it, take some water into the exam with you.

- Make sure you read and understand the rubric (instructions and rules) on the front of the exam paper.

- Allow some time at the start to read and consider the questions carefully before writing anything. Do not rush into answering before you have had a chance to think about it.

- Work out how much time you need to allocate to each question. During the exam try not to over-run on one question, leaving too little time for another.

For more tips on how to get the best from your revision and exams, see *Study Skills* by Elizabeth Holtom, published by Galore Park.

# Useful resources

All available from Galore Park: www.galorepark.co.uk.
*Preparing for Common Entrance Religious Studies* by Michael Wilcockson,
    ISBN: 9780903627603
*Study Skills* by Elizabeth Holtom, ISBN: 9781902984599

## Other titles

*Religious Studies for Common Entrance* by Susan Grenfell, ISBN: 9780340887905
*The Holy Bible* (The recommended translation is Today's New International Version
    but you can use any translation you like.)
*Seeking Religion: The Buddhist Experience* by Mel Thompson, ISBN: 9780340872475
*Seeking Religion: The Christian Experience* by JF Aylett and Kevin O'Donnell,
    ISBN: 9780340747681
*Seeking Religion: The Jewish Experience* by Liz Aylett and Kevin O'Donnell,
    ISBN: 9780340747735
*Seeking Religion: The Muslim Experience* by JF Aylett and Kevin O'Donnell,
    ISBN: 9780340747704
*Seeking Religion: The Sikh Experience* by Philip Emmett, ISBN: 9780340747728
*Seeking Religion: The Hindu Experience* by Liz Aylett and Kevin O'Donnell,
    ISBN: 9780340747698

# Chapter 1: Key words and ideas for Sections 1 and 2

This chapter lists the key words and ideas that may be tested in Sections 1 and 2 of the examination paper. Use the following list of words to test yourself. Cover up the right hand side of the page and see how much you can remember.

*These words in bold are the words set by the examination board, which can be tested in the short answer Part a questions.*

| | |
|---|---|
| **Ark of the Covenant** | A sacred box containing the two tablets of the Law (Ten Commandments). |
| **Atonement** | Getting back into a right relationship with God. |
| **Baal** | A Canaanite god. |
| **Baptism** | The symbolic washing away of sin. |
| **Blasphemy** | Speaking against God or making oneself equal to God. |
| **Blessed** | True happiness as given by God. |
| **Christ or Messiah** | Anointed one. |
| **Covenant** | An agreement between God and His people. |
| **Crucifixion** | The Roman death penalty of being nailed to a cross. |
| **Disciple** | A follower or student. |
| **Eden** | The garden in Genesis 2 where everything is perfect. |
| **Faith** | Having an active trust in someone or in God. |
| **Fasting** | Going without food to make a person more aware of God. |
| **Justice** | Treating others fairly. |
| **Miracle** | An act of God which breaks the laws of physics. |
| **Pacifist** | A person who refuses to fight or use violent force. |
| **Parable** | A story or saying comparing the Kingdom of God with everyday human events. |
| **Pharisee** | A Jewish religious teacher who taught strict obedience to the law. |

| | |
|---|---|
| **Prophet** | Someone chosen by God to speak God's message to people. |
| **Resurrection** | Rising to new life from the dead. |
| **Sabbath** | The Jewish day of rest. |
| **Sacrifice** | Giving up something for something of greater value. |
| **Salvation** | Being saved and brought into relationship with God. |
| **Sanhedrin** | The Jewish ruling council made up of 70 councillors and the High Priest. |
| **Sin** | Disobeying God and being separated from Him. |
| **Sinai/Horeb** | The mountain of God. |
| **Son of God** | The title describing Jesus' unique relationship with God. |
| **Son of Man** | The title describing Jesus' role as the one who would suffer for others. |
| **Stewardship** | Looking after the world for God. |
| **Temptation** | The desire to do something wrong. |
| **Transfiguration** | A change of Jesus' appearance. |
| **Wisdom** | The ability to distinguish between good and evil. |
| **Worship** | Giving God praise and honour. |

*Learn the following words and ideas to help you with the longer questions.*

## LOOK, SAY, COVER, WRITE, CHECK

| | |
|---|---|
| Abraham | Called by God to travel from Ur in Mesopotamia to settle in Canaan. God promised Abraham that he would have many descendents. Abraham was the first to believe in one God. |
| Adam | Created by God using dust of the earth. God breathed life into him. |
| Agape | The Greek word for love and is used to refer to the generous love Jesus frequently taught about. |
| Amaziah | King Jeroboam's priest at Bethel who told Amos to return home. |

| | |
|---|---|
| Amos | A prophet in 760 BC who warned the northern kingdom of God's judgement because of their slack religious and moral lifestyle. |
| Angels | God's messengers who are neither human nor divine. |
| Apostles | 'One who is sent' – refers to Jesus' disciples' role after his death preaching Christianity in and outside Palestine. |
| Baptism | The symbolic moment when sins are washed away and a person starts a new life. Jesus' baptism marked the start of his preaching ministry. |
| Beatitudes | Jesus' list of those who have the right attitude to others and to God and who will enter the Kingdom of God. |
| Cain and Abel | The sons of Adam and Eve. Cain grew crops and Abel looked after animals. Cain killed Abel. |
| Church | Refers to all Christians worldwide. Over the centuries the Church has divided itself into denominations such as the Roman Catholic, Orthodox and Protestant churches. |
| Cicely Saunders | 1918–2005. A doctor who pioneered helping those with terminal illnesses. She founded St Christopher's Hospice in 1967. She believed euthanasia is wrong because it does not respect a person's value and can cause families great distress. |
| Creationism | The belief that Genesis gives a reliable account of the origins of the universe and that evolutionary views are wrong. |
| David | Succeeded King Saul as king but, despite his greatness, had an affair with Bathsheba which the prophet Nathan strongly condemned. |
| Dietrich Bonhoeffer | 1906–1945. A German Lutheran pastor who had to choose between an academic career in the USA and helping in his Church against the Nazi regime under Hitler. He helped found the Confessing Church which trained people in secret. He was also involved in the plot to kill Hitler. The plotters were all sent to concentration camps and executed. He was hanged in 1945. |
| Elijah | The first great prophet during the time of King Ahab. At Mount Carmel he showed that God was greater than the Canaanite god Baal. |

| | |
|---|---|
| Euthanasia | Means literally 'a good death' and is when a person asks a doctor to help them to die (usually because they are very ill). |
| Eve | Created from Adam using one of his ribs. |
| Evolution | The scientific belief that all life forms have evolved from simpler forms. |
| Fair Trade | An international movement which makes sure that producers in poorer countries are paid a fair deal for their products (such as coffee and chocolate). |
| Gamaliel | An influential lawyer or rabbi who persuaded the Sanhedrin to release the Apostles from prison. |
| Hypocrisy | Saying one thing but doing another, or pretending outwardly to believe something but actually believing something else. |
| Jackie Pullinger | Born 1944. Felt called by God to work in the Walled City in Hong Kong. She founded a youth club to help those with drug addiction. |
| James and John | Fishermen who became Jesus' disciples and asked Jesus to give them important places in the Kingdom of God. |
| Jezebel | The wife of King Ahab who encouraged the worship of the Canaanite god Baal. |
| Jonathan | Saul's son and a great friend of David. |
| Kingdom of God | God's rule on earth and a future perfect state (heaven). |
| Martin Luther King | 1929–1968. A black Baptist minister who led a movement to overcome the unjust laws which segregated blacks and whites in the USA. He believed in non-violent protest and arranged a bus boycott, demonstrations and a march of thousands to Washington. He was assassinated in 1968. |
| Martyrdom | The example set by some when they are prepared to die for their beliefs. |
| Mary Magdalene | One of Jesus' closest women followers, the first to arrive at Jesus' tomb and meet the resurrected Jesus. |
| Meg Guillebaud | Born 1943. Brought up in Rwanda but was ordained a priest in Britain. She returned in 1995 to help in a country torn apart by the massacre of the Tutsi people by the Hutsu tribe. She helped people from both groups |

by reconciling them to each other and overcoming their prejudices and fears.

| | |
|---|---|
| Miracle on the River Kwai | A book by Ernest Gordon which describes how a British prisoner of war in Japan working on the Burma railway allowed himself to be killed by a guard to save the lives of hundreds of others. This happened when the guard thought a prisoner had stolen a spade. |
| Moses | Led the children of Israel out of Egypt and was given the Law (or Torah) by God at Sinai. |
| Mother Teresa | 1910–1997. An Irish Catholic nun who moved to India to help the homeless and poorest people in Calcutta. She started schools and a special town for lepers and founded Nirmal Hriday to help the dying. |
| Oscar Romero | 1917–1980. A Catholic archbishop of San Salvador, Latin America. He became aware of the great gap between the very rich land owners and the poor who lived in slums. He sided with the poor and spoke for them. This made him enemies in the Church and with the government. He was shot saying mass in 1980. |
| Paranormal experiences | Experiences of having visions of people who have died, or near death experiences where the soul leaves the body for a while at death and returns shortly afterwards. |
| Pentecost | A Jewish festival but was also the time when the Apostles received the Holy Spirit. Pentecost in Christian terms is the birth of the Church. |
| Persecution | Being imprisoned, unfairly treated and even killed for one's beliefs. |
| Peter | One of Jesus' closest disciples and although he denied knowing Jesus, he eventually became the first leader of the Church. |
| Pilate | The Roman governor who condemned Jesus to death by crucifixion. |
| Racism | An irrational hatred of people of other races. This can led to discrimination, persecution and even killing. |
| Ransom | The way Jesus described his role as a sacrifice to 'pay off' the punishment for human sin and bring humans back to God. |

| | |
|---|---|
| Reconciliation | Helping people overcome their differences and be united to one another. In Christian terms it also refers to Jesus' death which brought humans back into relationship with God. |
| Redemption | The state of forgiveness and being at one with God. |
| Saul | A king in ancient Israel who suffered from depression and was jealous of David's success. |
| Sermon on the Plain | Where Jesus gave some of his most important moral and religious teaching, e.g. on loving one's enemies and the importance of forgiveness. |
| Ten Commandments | The 10 basic religious and moral laws given to Moses at Sinai. |
| The Good Samaritan | Samaritans were despised by many Jews but in Jesus' parable a Samaritan is the only one who truly carries out God's command to love one's neighbour. |
| The Lost Son | In Jesus' parable the younger son is an example of one who repents and is forgiven by God. |
| The serpent | Represents doubt and uncertainty in the Garden of Eden. He suggests that Eve should eat from the tree of knowledge. |
| The Sower and the Seed | In Jesus' parable the different types of ground refer to the way in which Christianity is received by different people. |
| The Temple | The most sacred building in ancient Israel. It was started by David, completed by Solomon, destroyed in 586 BC and built again by Herod the Great in the time of Jesus. |
| Transfiguration | Refers to the time when Jesus' body was transformed, the disciples saw him in his divine state and realised he was God's Son. |
| Trevor Huddleston | 1913–1998. An Anglican priest who worked in a township outside Johannesburg, South Africa. He campaigned against apartheid which segregated blacks from whites and campaigned for better housing and education for black people. He was an active supporter of the ANC (African National Congress) which managed to abolish apartheid. |

| | |
|---|---|
| Turin shroud | An ancient cloth with the image of a crucified man burnt on it but as a negative image. Many think Jesus was buried in it and the image was caused by the power of the resurrection. |
| Zacchaeus | A tax collector who after meeting Jesus promised not to cheat people and offered to pay back everything he had stolen with interest. |

## Summary

You should now know the following:

1. The main words to be tested in the short answer Part a questions.

2. The main words and ideas used in the longer questions.

# Chapter 2: Old Testament texts and contemporary issues

There are twelve texts in this chapter, which may be tested in Section 1 of the examination paper. Have a copy of the Bible to hand and read the relevant verses noted at the beginning of each section.

## 2.1 The Creation

Read: *Genesis 1: 1–2: 25*

### Short questions

From the official vocabulary list, questions might be asked such as:

Q.   What is stewardship?

A.   Looking after the world for God.

Q.   What is the Sabbath?

A.   Jewish day of rest.

### Summary points of the story

In the **First Creation** story:

- In the beginning God created the heavens and the earth.

- Nothing had any shape or form.
  - The **1st day** God created **light**, which he called day.
  - The **2nd day** God **separated the waters** and created the **sky**.
  - The **3rd day** God created **land**, **seas** and **plants**.
  - The **4th day** God created the **stars**, the **sun** and **moon**.
  - The **5th day** God created **birds** and **sea creatures**.
  - The **6th day** God created **land animals**. He created **human beings** in his **own image**.

- God gave humans **responsibility** over all creatures.

- God commanded humans to **increase** and **rule** the earth.

- God completed his work on the **7th day** and **rested**. He made this a holy day.

In the **Second Creation** story:

- Before any shrub had appeared God created **man** or Adam.

- God made **Adam** from the **dust of the earth** and **breathed** life into him.

- God planted a garden called **Eden**.

- In the middle of Eden there were **two trees**; the tree of **life** and the tree of **knowledge** of good and evil.

- God placed Adam in Eden and told him to care for it but **not to eat** from the tree of knowledge.

- God created a **helper, Eve,** for Adam so he should not be alone.

- God put Adam into a deep sleep and took one of his **ribs**, from which he created woman or **Eve**.

## Key ideas

Most scholars think that the two creation stories were written at different times and therefore make slightly different points.

The **First Creation** story teaches that there is a God-given order and design of the universe:

- God is a majestic **creator** and creates just by **commanding**.

- Humans are given control over creation because they are made in **God's image** and share in his power.

- Humans have a responsibility to **steward** and maintain the God-given order of the world.

- Everything has its proper **place** in the creation.

The **Second Creation** story concentrates on humans and their relationship with God:

- The relationship between man and God is based on **love**. God cares enough for man to provide him with a companion, woman.

- God only breathes into man not other creatures because it shows how much **humans share in God's nature**.

- Men and women have **a natural sexual attraction** to each other which is why they marry and have children.

# Contemporary issues and evaluation

The following sample questions are provided with the points you need to consider in your answer.

## (i) Science and creation

*Sample question*

**Q.** Do modern theories of the origins of the universe such as the Big Bang contradict Genesis?

*Points to consider:*

**On the one hand...** some agree that because the creation happened by **chance**, there is no need for God.

**On the other hand...** Others argue that **God** could have been the cause of the Big Bang.

*Sample question*

**Q.** Does evolution suggest that humans are not specially created by God?

*Points to consider:*

**On the one hand...** some argue that humans could have evolved as part of **God's plan**; evolution does not necessarily suggest humans are not special.

**On the other hand...** others disagree because they believe there is **no firm evidence** that humans evolved from lower life forms and that God must have specially created such an intelligent animal.

*Sample question*

**Q.** Does modern science contradict the Bible?

*Points to consider:*

**On the one hand...** some Christian 'creationists' argue that science is less trustworthy than the Bible as science has not proved where we come from, Genesis explains things better.

**On the other hand... progressive** Christians argue that science tells us **how** things might have happened, but religious beliefs explain **why** things happen in terms of purpose and meaning.

**Your turn**

Now try the sample questions on the previous pages for yourself.

### (ii) Stewardship and the environment

**Sample question**

**Q.** Should we try to reduce global warming?

*Points to consider:*

**On the one hand…** some argue that the teachings of Genesis may be interpreted that we should make every effort to reduce **global warming** through recycling, reduction of carbon gases, etc.

**On the other hand…** others argue that the **world has undergone many changes** in the past and that global warming is making us scared for no good reason.

---

**Sample question**

**Q.** Is it wrong to experiment on animals to develop medicines?

*Points to consider:*

**On the one hand…** some argue that this is **exploiting** the weak and causing unnecessary suffering.

**On the other hand…** others argue that it is not against the principle of stewardship to **experiment on animals** to develop medicines and cures for illnesses.

---

**Your turn**

Now try the sample questions on the previous pages for yourself.

## 2.2 The nature of man and the fall

Read: *Genesis 3*

### Short questions

From the official vocabulary list, questions might be asked such as:

Q.  What is sin?

A.  Disobeying God and being separated from Him.

### Summary points of the story

- The **serpent** tempted the woman to eat from the **Tree of Knowledge**.
  - The serpent told Eve that she would not die if she ate from the tree but she would become like God and **know good and evil**.

- **Eve** took some **fruit** from the tree and ate it.
  - She gave some to Adam.
  - When they ate it they became aware they were **naked** and they made themselves clothes.

- When they **heard God** walking in the garden they **hid**.
  - Adam said to God they had hidden because they were naked.
  - God asked him whether he had eaten from the Tree of Knowledge.
  - **Adam** said that Eve had given him some fruit from it.
  - Eve said the serpent had deceived her.

- God **punished** the **serpent** by making him crawl on his belly and caused **humans** to be scared of him and try to kill him.

- God punished the woman by making **childbirth** painful and making her husband **rule over her**.

- God punished the man by making **work painful**.

- God made clothes for Adam and Eve and then **expelled** them from the Garden of Eden.

- God protected the **Tree of Life** by placing cherubim and a flashing sword round it.

## Key ideas

- **Eden** means 'delight' and describes a paradise where everyone and everything works in **harmony**.

- Eating from the **Tree of Knowledge** means being or able to survive on one's own without being **obedient** to God.

- Only God can be self made without creating evil. Humans are unable to have this knowledge and remain good.

- The **serpent** symbolises **human desire, rebelliousness, deceitfulness**.

- Eve's act symbolises human **desire for power**.

- Adam's act symbolises human **weakness** as he gives in to Eve.

- **Nakedness** symbolises **shame** and **conscience**, Adam and Eve know what they have done is wrong.

- The **punishments** symbolise the effects of **sin**. Sin means to cut one's self off from God, which is why Adam and Eve are **expelled** from Eden.

- The physical punishments symbolise the **pain** and suffering of ordinary life; the **inequality** of men and women's relationships; the **struggle** between humans and nature to survive.

## Contemporary issues and evaluation

*Sample question*

**Q.** Are men and women equal?

*Points to consider:*

**On the one hand...** some argue that men and women are equal because they are both equally **intelligent** and, given the same opportunities, both can achieve the same results.

**On the other hand...** others argue that because men and women are physically different men and women have very different **emotions. They are not equal and should be treated differently**.

*Sample question*

**Q.** Are we always responsible for the consequences of our actions?

*Points to consider:*

**On the one hand...** some say that as humans have **free will** they must always take the blame for their bad actions.

**On the other hand...** others say that human nature is **flawed** and as we are weak-willed we cannot always be blamed for the bad things we do.


*Sample question*

**Q.** Are humans naturally generous?

*Points to consider:*

**On the one hand...** some argue for a **liberal** view. Humans are good but it is their environment and upbringing which **distorts** their naturally good nature.

**On the other hand...** others consider that all humans are **deeply selfish**. Humans never perform entirely generous actions.


*Sample question*

**Q.** Is obedience to those in authority always good?

*Points to consider:*

**On the one hand...** some feel that if we fail to carry out the commands of those in authority then society might fall into **chaos**.

**On the other hand...** others argue obedience is only good if the **cause** is good. Obedience to a bad command is not justified.

**Your turn**

Now try the sample questions above for yourself.

# 2.3 Cain and Abel

Read: *Genesis 4: 1–16*

## Short questions

From the official vocabulary list, questions might be asked such as:

Q. What is sin?

A. Disobeying God and being separated from Him.

Q. What is sacrifice?

A. Giving up something for something of greater value.

## Summary points of the story

- **Eve** gave birth to **Cain** and **Abel**.
  - Abel was a **shepherd**.
  - Cain grew **crops**.
- **Abel** offered sacrifices of **animals** to God which **God was pleased with**.
- **Cain** offered sacrifices of **crops** to God which **did not please God**.
  - **Cain** was **angry**.
  - God told Cain to control his anger otherwise sin, which was '**crouching at the door**' would overcome him.

- In the field **Cain killed Abel**.
  - When God asked Cain where his brother was, Cain answered that he was not his '**brother's keeper**'.
  - God replied that Abel's blood was crying from the ground and he would therefore **punish** Cain by making it impossible for him to grow crops successfully.
  - God punished Cain more by making him **wander the earth**.
- However, God **protected** Cain from being killed by placing a '**mark**' on him.

## Key ideas

- Cain and Abel offer **sacrifices** as signs of their gratitude to God.

- God **rejects** Cain's offering because Cain's **motives** are bad. He was often angry and selfish.

- **Sin** is described like a demon waiting to pounce. Today this might be described in **psychological** terms to mean Cain has deep-seated anger.

- **Abel's blood** crying out refers to his **innocence**. Blood is also a symbol of **life**.

- The story teaches us a lot about the **nature of God**. God knows human thoughts and motives. He **desires** genuine worship from the heart. He punishes **fairly** (Cain could have been killed for the murder of Abel). He **cares** for the innocent. He **generously** gives people second chances.

- Cain's **wandering** explains the problems encountered in ancient societies between **city dwellers** and **nomads**.

## Contemporary issues and evaluation

---

*Sample question*

**Q.** Should murderers receive the death penalty?

*Points to consider:*

**On the one hand...** some argue that as punishments must **fit the crime** then the death penalty is reasonable and fair.

**On the other hand...** others argue that people must be given **second chances**. All life is sacred even those who commit terrible crimes should not be killed.

---

*Sample question*

**Q.** Is jealousy always bad?

*Points to consider:*

**On the one hand...** some feel that jealousy can make people act in selfish and **foolish** ways. It might even destroy them.

**On the other hand...** others feel that jealousy can be sometimes **channelled** into working harder to succeed and achieve great things.

---

*Sample question*

**Q.** Do humans ever act with entirely pure motives?

*Points to consider:*

**On the one hand...** some people think that even if this is true many try to **overcome** their flaws and act for pure motives. **God's generous** nature acknowledges this.

**On the other hand...** others argue that it is in our nature to **survive**, so our motives are always mixed.

**Your turn**

Now try the sample questions on the previous pages for yourself.

# 2.4 The near sacrifice of Isaac

Read: *Genesis 22: 1–19*

## Short questions

From the official vocabulary list, questions might be asked such as:

Q. What is sacrifice?

A. Giving up something for something of greater value.

## Summary points of the story

- God decided to **test Abraham**.

- Abraham was told to take **Isaac** to Mount Moriah and **sacrifice** him as a burnt offering.

- Early in the morning Abraham set off with wood to make the fire for the burnt sacrifice.

- He left the servants behind and took Isaac to worship God.

- Isaac **carried the wood** and Abraham took the **knife**.

- Isaac asked why if they had wood and fire there was **no lamb** for the sacrifice.

- Abraham said **God would provide** the lamb.

- Abraham built the altar, **bound Isaac** and put him on top of the wood.

- As he was about to kill Isaac, an **angel** told him to stop and that God now knew of Abraham's faith.

- Abraham saw a **ram caught by its horns in a bush** and he offered the ram as a sacrifice instead.

- The angel called a second time that God would bless Abraham and make his **descendents as numerous as stars** in the sky and sand on the seashore.

- God also promised that he would give Abraham **land**.

## Key ideas

- There were many kinds of **sacrifices** in the ancient world. A sacrifice was means of pleasing or thanking God using food, produce or an animal.

- An **animal sacrifice** was the greatest offering because its **blood** represented **life**.

- An **atonement sacrifice** was a special sacrifice to God in the hope that he would **forgive the sins** of a person or people.

- God's command of Abraham is a **test**: it tests his **obedience** to God; it tests whether he is prepared to make the **ultimate sacrifice** of his son as a form of animal sacrifice.

- The action of the **angel** shows that atonement sacrifices should be based on **genuine faith**.

- The **covenant** of people and land is God's **promise** and reward for faith.

- **God's voice** might be explained today as our **conscience**.

## Contemporary issues and evaluation

*Sample question*

**Q.** Should we always obey our conscience?

*Points to consider:*

**On the one hand...** some argue, such as **Bonhoeffer**, that some situations are so **evil**, such as Hitler's killing of the Jews, that obedience to conscience means disobeying the law for the **greater good**.

**On the other hand...** others argue that conscience is **unreliable** and could just be our own **selfish desires** 'speaking' to us. If we all behaved like Bonhoeffer law and order would **break down**.

**Your turn**

Now try the sample questions above for yourself.

# 2.5 The Ten Commandments

Read: *Exodus 19: 1–8; Exodus 20: 1–20*

## Short questions

From the official vocabulary list, questions might be asked such as:

Q.   What is meant by covenant?

A.   Agreement between God and his people.

Q.   What is meant by Sabbath?

A.   Jewish day of rest.

Q. What is Sinai?

A. Mountain of God.

Q. What is sin?

A. Disobeying God and being separated from Him.

## Summary points of the story

- In the Sinai desert God called **Moses** up the **mountain**.

- Moses is to tell the Israelites how God rescued them from Egypt on '**eagles' wings**'.

- They are to keep God's covenant and become a **holy nation**.

- Moses went down the mountain and gave the Israelites God's words.

- When Moses went up the mountain again, God gave Moses the **Ten Commandments**:

  1. You shall have **no other gods**;
  2. You shall **not make any idols**;
  3. You shall **not misuse God's name**;
  4. You shall keep the **Sabbath day holy** by working six days and resting on the 7th;
  5. You shall **honour your father and mother**;
  6. You shall **not murder**;
  7. You shall **not commit adultery**;
  8. You shall **not steal**;
  9. You shall **not give false witness**;
  10. You shall **not envy or covet** (your neighbour's wife, his servants, his possessions).

- The **people** were **afraid** when they saw the smoke and thunder from Mount Sinai.

- Moses told them not to be afraid, this was a **test** from God to stop them from **sinning**.

## Key ideas

- The Ten Commandments form the heart of God's **covenant** with Israel.

- A **holy nation** means a nation which is specially chosen by God to be an example to the world.

- God has rescued Israel from Egypt as a sign of his **love**.

- The commandments are the 10 most important of the **613 commandments** of the law which God gives to Moses.

- The commandments are in **two tables**: 1–4 are **religious duties**; 5–10 are **moral duties**.

- **Commandment 1**: Judaism is a **monotheism** (worship of one God) which also means there is only **one form of morality** (knowing what is good and bad).

- **Commandment 2**: as God is **not a thing** then **no earthly thing** or human-made thing can be a source of power or **authority**.

- **Commandment 3**: making a **promise** (using God's name) means it **cannot be broken**. Misusing God's name is also called blasphemy: that is making oneself equal or greater than God.

- **Commandment 4**: remembers God's **creation** and stops the **exploitation** of workers by giving them a day of rest.

- **Commandment 5**: recognises parents as a source of **wisdom** and **authority**.

- **Commandment 6**: life is **sacred** because it is God-given. **Deliberate killing**, unless authorised by God, (as in war or capital punishment) is **morally wrong**.

- **Commandment 7**: **wives** were seen as the **property of husbands**, so adultery is a form of theft.

- **Commandment 8**: stealing destroys people's **livelihood** and **trust** of one another. The heart of the covenant is trust.

- **Commandment 9**: as many crimes were punished using the **death penalty,** making a false statement about someone was serious.

- **Commandment 10**: in small communities **respect for property** is essential; envy breaks down **trust** and stability of society.

## Contemporary issues and evaluation

*Sample question*

**Q.** Should the aim of punishment be to deter others?

*Points to consider:*

**On the one hand...** some argue that unless punishments are **severe** then no one will take them **seriously**.

**On the other hand...** others say that the aim of punishment is to **reform** those who have done wrong so that they become **good members** of society again.

**Q.** Should the aim of punishment be to make wrong-doers suffer?

*Points to consider:*

**On the one hand...** some agree that punishment should cause suffering to the wrong-doer so that the people who have suffered from a crime can **feel justice** has been carried out.

**On the other hand...** others argue that many (including Jesus and Gandhi) feel that retribution makes society **morally weak**. True justice comes from **compassion**.

---

*Sample question*

**Q.** Should murderers always receive the death penalty?

*Points to consider:*

**On the one hand...** some argue that as punishments must **fit the crime** then the death penalty is reasonable and fair. An eye for an eye.

**On the other hand...** others argue that people must be given **second chances**. It does not allow for repentance and it degrades society.

---

*Sample question*

**Q.** Is the most important right the right to life?

*Points to consider:*

**On the one hand...** some argue that the right to life is the **basis** for many other rights such as respect for property, the right to free speech etc because the right to life means having a good **quality** of life.

**On the other hand...** others think that this is too vague and that rights have to be based on other things such as **freedom**, **happiness** and **protection**. An example of this is in the **United Nations Declaration of Human Rights**.

---

 **Your turn**

Now try the sample questions above for yourself.

## 2.6 David and Jonathan

Read: *1 Samuel 20*

### Short questions

From the official vocabulary list, questions might be asked such as:

Q.  What is faith?

A.  Having an active trust in someone or in God.

### Summary points of the story

- **David** went to **Jonathan** for protection from **Saul** because he thought he had upset him.

- Jonathan promised to help David.

- David asked Jonathan to tell Saul that if he asked why he was not at the New Moon festival dinner he was to tell him that he **had to go to Bethlehem** to make the annual family sacrifice.

- If **Saul then lost his temper** then he would know he was angry with him and Jonathan was to kill him.

- Jonathan said he would find out what his father thought.

- He would not let any harm come to David because of his **love and friendship** for him.

- Jonathan said that at the festival when David is hiding in the field he would give David a sign:
  - if he **shot three arrows to one side** of him then he is **safe**;
  - if he shot three arrows **behind him** he is in **danger** and must get away.

- On the **first day** of the festival Saul thought David was missing because he must be unclean for the ceremonies.

- On the **second day** Jonathan explained to Saul that David had to go to Bethlehem.

- **Saul was very angry** and commanded Jonathan to bring David to him so he could kill him.

- Jonathan tried to explain that David had done no wrong to Saul, but **Saul threw his spear at him**.

- Jonathan went out and shot his **arrows behind** David.

- David and Jonathan **embraced each other and swore friendship** to each other.

## Key ideas

- **King Saul** and **David** had been **friends** because David had killed **Goliath** the champion of Israel's enemy the Philistines, and helped Saul in other battles.

- But Saul was now **jealous** of David because of his success in battle and now he wanted to get rid of him.

- David had become very good **friends** with Saul's son **Jonathan**.

- Jonathan acts as the **mediator** or go-between between his father and David.

- At the **New Moon Festival** it was traditional for families to be together.

- David used the festival as a **test**: if Saul did not react badly then he would know that Saul was not angry with him.

- Jonathan shows great **bravery** and **loyalty** in protecting his friend.

## Contemporary issues and evaluation

*Sample question*

**Q.** Is loyalty to country more important than loyalty to friends?

*Points to consider:*

**On the one hand...** some argue that loyalty to country must come first because without law and order then ordinary life is impossible.

**On the other hand...** others think that without loyalty to our friends we lose sense of our most important values: love, trust and companionship.

*Sample question*

**Q.** Is charity more important than friendship?

*Points to consider:*

**On the one hand...** some argue that the example of **Mother Teresa** in Calcutta showed that helping the poor and weak and putting others before one's self is more important.

**On the other hand...** others argue that what motivated Mother Teresa was friendship for the poor. She placed **love** for **humanity first**. Charity is a result of friendship.

**Sample question**

**Q.** Is racism the result of jealousy?

**Points to consider:**

**On the one hand...** some argue that racism is caused by many factors but often by **fear** and jealousy that one group is taking away lands, jobs, values, etc.

**On the other hand...** others argue that **Trevor Huddleson's** example in South Africa showed that apartheid was based on irrational ideas of prejudice and a failure to see black people as made in the **image of God**.

 **Your turn**

Now try the sample questions above for yourself.

## 2.7 David and Bathsheba and Nathan's parable

Read: 2 Samuel 11: 1–17; 2 Samuel 12: 1–14

### Short questions

From the official vocabulary list, questions might be asked such as:

Q. What is sin?

A. Disobeying God and being separated from Him.

Q. What is a prophet?

A. Someone chosen by God to speak God's message to people.

Q. What is a parable?

A. A story with a moral using everyday events.

Q. What is temptation?

A. The desire to do something wrong.

### Summary points of the story

David and Bathsheba:

- One evening in spring **David** could see a **beautiful woman bathing** on her roof.

- He found out that she was **Bathsheba,** wife of **Uriah the Hittite**.

- David had sex with her and then, later, he found she was **pregnant**.

- David told **Joab** to send **Uriah** home to report on the war to him.

- He hoped he would **sleep** with Bathsheba but Uriah slept at the **door of the palace**.

- Uriah said he could not go home whilst his **men were fighting**.

- The next evening David got Uriah **drunk**, but Uriah **slept with the servants**.

- David sent a letter to Joab telling him to place Uriah in the **front line of the battle** and then to withdraw his troops so Uriah would be killed.

- Joab did as he was told and **Uriah was killed**.

Nathan's parable:

- God sent **Nathan** to **David** to tell him a parable.
    - In the parable there were two men, **one rich** and **one poor**.
    - The rich man had a **lot of sheep** but the poor man had only **one little ewe lamb**.
    - The ewe lamb was loved and part of the family, '**it was like a daughter to him**'.
    - One day the rich man had to entertain a traveller but he did not want to use his own sheep so **he took the poor man's lamb** and prepared it for dinner.

- When David heard the parable he was very angry and said the **rich man should die**.

- Nathan said, '**You are that man!**'.

- Nathan told David that as king he should not have killed Uriah and slept with Bathsheba.

- God would now punish David: he would see his wives taken away by one of his friends.

- David confessed that he had **sinned**.

- Nathan said that **God** would now **forgive** him; he would not die, but his **son would die instead**.

## Key ideas

- The proper role of the king was to **protect**, to be a '**shepherd** of the people'.

- David's affair with Bathsheba shows his **misuse of power**.

- David is ruled by **lust** and emotion **not reason** when he sends Uriah to his death.

- **Uriah's** character **contrasts** to **David**: he is loyal, trustworthy and loving.

- David's suggestion of the **death penalty** for the wrong doer in the parable shows how much he feels injustice was done. The usual punishment would have been a **fine**.

- David's violent son, **Absolom**, was later killed when he fought against his father.

## Contemporary issues and evaluation

*Sample question*

**Q.** Should one always obey the law even if the law is bad?

*Points to consider:*

**On the one hand...** some argue that we do not always have the bigger picture and to disobey the law whenever we feel like might lead to **anarchy**. Uriah obeyed David for this reason.

**On the other hand...** others argue that we should protest against unfair laws. **Martin Luther King** led a campaign of **civil disobedience** in America because of the laws which discriminated against black people, and in the end he won.

*Sample question*

**Q.** Should leaders and figures of authority be punished more if they misuse their power?

*Points to consider:*

**On the one hand...** some think that they should be punished more because more authority means **greater responsibility**. If this responsibility is abused then the punishment should be greater.

**On the other hand...** others argue that the **law** and **punishments** apply to all people **equally**. Although Harold Shipman killed many patients he was not condemned to death but imprisoned as the law demands.

**Your turn**

Now try the sample questions on the previous page for yourself.

# 2.8 Solomon's wisdom

Read: *1 Kings 3*

## Short questions

From the official vocabulary list, questions might be asked such as:

Q. What is the Ark of the Covenant?

A. A sacred box containing the two tablets of the Law (Ten Commandments).

Q. What is wisdom?

A. The ability to distinguish between good and evil.

Q. What is justice?

A. Treating others fairly.

## Summary points of the story

- **Solomon** kept to the **laws of God** except that he continued to make **sacrifices at the shrines**.

- One day at the shrine of **Gibeon** God appeared to him in a **dream**.

  - God asked Solomon to request whatever he would most like.

  - Solomon said that he would like a '**discerning heart**' to be able to see what was right and what was wrong.

  - God was pleased and said he would grant his request so Solomon would be able to rule **justly**.

- Furthermore, because he had not asked for them he would give him great **riches and a long life**.

- Solomon returned to **Jerusalem** and made an offering at the **Ark of the Covenant**.

- One day **two prostitutes** came to Solomon both claiming that a baby was their own.

  - One claimed that the other had accidentally lain on her own baby and suffocated it and then stolen her baby.

  - She had put the dead baby in place of hers.

  - Solomon told them to bring a sword and then ordered for **the baby to be chopped in two**.

  - The **real mother** shouted out for him to stop and let the other woman keep the baby.

  - The false mother told the king to carry on so that neither of them could have the baby.

  - Solomon gave the baby to the true mother.

- Everyone was amazed by Solomon's **wisdom** and **justice**.

## Key ideas

- **Solomon** was **King David's son** and famous for his great **wealth**, wisdom and building the **Temple**.

- His **sacrifice** at Gibeon and later in Jerusalem shows that Solomon was a **religious man**.

- **Dreams** in the ancient world were thought to be the means by which **God spoke** to humans.

- God **tests** Solomon by offering him whatever he would like.

- Solomon asks for the ability to know the **difference** between good and bad.

- **Riches** and long life are signs of God's **blessing**.

- Solomon's judgement shows his ability and **skill** to **understand** human nature; the true mother would never kill her own child.

- **Prostitutes** were low on the social scale but Solomon **judged them fairly**.

- Solomon's shows that **wisdom** is: **skill, understanding**, being open to **God's will**, putting **others first**, being **fair**.

## Contemporary issues and evaluation

*Sample question*

**Q.** Is having wisdom more than just being good?

*Points to consider:*

**On the one hand...** some think that wisdom is the ability to be just and fair. A wise choice is having the ability to know what moral principles to use in a situation.

**On the other hand...** others think that having wisdom is being skilful. A wise choice is good because it works. It could be based on cunning or even a lie.

*Sample question*

**Q.** Is a good leader one who puts other people first?

*Points to consider:*

**On the one hand...** some argue that this is true because a leader has to use his **talents** to **serve** others first. Solomon treated the needs of two prostitutes wisely.

**On the other hand...** others think that a leader is there to put the law, justice, business or the cause first. For example, a businessman has to make his business a **success**, otherwise everyone loses.

 **Your turn**

Now try the sample questions above for yourself.

# 2.9 Elijah and the prophets of Baal

Read: *1 Kings 18*

## Short questions

From the official vocabulary list, questions might be asked such as:

Q.  What is a prophet?

A.  Someone chosen by God to speak God's message to people.

Q.  Who is Baal?

A.  A Canaanite god.

Q.  What is a sacrifice?

A.  Giving up something for something of greater value.

## Summary points of the story

- King **Ahab** sent the prophet **Obadiah** to **find water** during a terrible drought and famine.

- Obadiah met Elijah. **Elijah** told him to report to Ahab that he had met him.

- **Obadiah** was **scared** that Ahab would kill him if Elijah did not then present himself to the King.

- Elijah assured him that he would meet the King.

- When Ahab met Elijah, **Ahab** said, 'Is that you, you **troubler of Israel**?'.

- Elijah replied that the real troubler was Ahab.

- Elijah challenged **450 prophets of Baal** and 400 **prophets of Asherah** to contest at **Mount Carmel**.

- Elijah told the people that they had to **choose** between worship of **God** or the worship of **Baal**.

- Two bulls were cut in pieces and placed on two piles of wood but not set alight.

- Whichever **god set the pile alight** would be the **true god**.

- The prophets of Baal called on their god, but nothing happened.

- Elijah teased them and told them to shout louder to **wake up Baal**. But nothing happened.

- Elijah built an altar of **12 stones** (one for each of the 12 Tribes of Israel) and then poured **four jars of water** on the wood.

- They poured water three times.

- Elijah prayed to God; then God sent **fire to consume the sacrifice**.

- The people shouted, 'The Lord – he is God!'.

- Elijah commanded that the prophets of **Baal should be killed**.

- **Elijah** went to **pray** at the top of **Mount Carmel**.

- It began to **rain** heavily.

### Key ideas

- The drought had **lasted over three years,** so many had turned to worship the **Canaanite** god **Baal** who was the **god of rain**.

- **Elijah** was Israel's greatest **prophet** and believed that **only God** should be worshipped.

- **Waking up Baal** was part of usual Canaanite worship but Elijah used it to **tease** the prophets.

- The **12 stones** Elijah used symbolised the **whole nation** (ten tribes in the south and two in the north).

- Elijah's prayer is **simple** compared to the other prophets.

- The people's cry is the most important **Jewish prayer**, that God is one.

- Elijah kills the prophets of Baal to **stop rumours** that Baal had lit his sacrifice and as a sign of God's **judgement** of **false worship**.

## Contemporary issues and evaluation

### Sample question

**Q.** Should violence be used to defend one's beliefs?

### Points to consider:

**On the one hand...** some think that in some extreme cases it is right to defend one's beliefs against those who would **harm** or even kill you themselves. Use of force is also a **symbol** of the power of belief.

**On the other hand...** others think that the use of violence never really persuades people. **Oscar Romero** believed that change comes through people acting together. Defending one's beliefs might mean having to die for them, as he did.

### Sample question

**Q.** Are celebrities today's false gods?

### Points to consider:

**On the one hand...** some think that this is true because **no celebrity can ever live up to people's hopes and expectations**. They do not bring people real happiness.

**On the other hand...** others think that we like to see successful people. It **gives us hope** and they show us what humans can achieve. They are only false when they **misuse their success**.

 **Your turn**

Now try the sample questions above for yourself.

## 2.10 Elijah and the still small voice

Read: *1 Kings 19: 1–18*

### Short questions

From the official vocabulary list, questions might be asked such as:

Q. What is a prophet?

A. Someone chosen by God to speak God's message to people.

Q. What is Horeb?

A. The mountain of God.

Q. What is meant by covenant?

A. Agreement between God and His people.

Q. Who is Baal?

A. A Canaanite god.

### Summary points of the story

- When **Jezebel** heard how **Elijah** had **killed** the **prophets of Baal** she threatened to kill him.
- Elijah fled to the wilderness. He had had enough and prayed to God to let him die.
  - An angel woke him up and he **found a cake and a jar of water**.
  - The angel woke him again and told him to eat again for the journey.
- Elijah came to **Horeb** and **stayed in a cave**.
- God visited Elijah and asked him what he was doing.
- Elijah answered that he was the only true prophet left and now the Israelites were trying to kill him.
- God told him to stand on the mountain because He was going to '**pass by**'.
- Then a powerful **wind** blew which broke rocks – but God was not in the wind.
- Then there was an **earthquake** – but God was not in the earthquake.
- Then there was **fire** – but God was not in the fire.
- Then there was a **gentle whisper** (a still small voice) and it asked Elijah what he was doing.
- Elijah replied he had tried very hard to make the people keep to the **covenant**.
- God told him to return and **anoint two kings**.
- He also told him to anoint **Elisha**.
- God told Elijah that He had protected 7000 people from worshipping Baal.

## Key ideas

- **Jezebel** was the **wife** of King **Ahab**. She **encouraged** the worship of **Baal**, the chief god of the Canaanites.

- Elijah was **depressed** because God had not stopped Jezebel killing God's prophets.

- **Horeb** is a special mountain where God has **revealed** himself in the past.

- Unlike his experience with the prophets of Baal, God is **not found in nature** (wind, fire, earthquake).

- God is found in one's **heart**, in one's **thoughts** and in **stillness**.

- **Elisha** continued Elijah's work after **Elijah died** and was taken to heaven.

## Contemporary issues and evaluation

*Sample question*

**Q.** Does God only speak to us when we are lonely?

*Points to consider:*

**On the one hand...** some argue that it is when we are lonely or sad that we are most **receptive** to God's presence. If **God is love** then we have be aware of this in quiet or **prayer**.

**On the other hand...** others argue that God can equally be experienced when we are lonely but **intellectually** when we think about the cause of the universe or the beauty and **design of nature**.

*Sample question*

**Q.** How can we know when God is acting in the world?

*Points to consider:*

**On the one hand...** some argue that we can know when God acts because as God is **good** then an event which God **causes** will always produce good.

**On the other hand...** others argue that it is very hard to know. An earthquake might **equally** be God's punishment or just an **unfortunate event** in nature.

**Your turn**

Now try the sample questions on the previous page for yourself.

# 2.11 Amos' message

Read: *Amos 5*

## Short questions

From the official vocabulary list, questions might be asked such as:

Q.   What is a prophet?

A.   Someone chosen by God to speak God's message to people.

Q.   What is meant by justice?

A.   Treating others fairly.

Q.   What is worship?

A.   Giving God praise and honour.

## Summary points of the story

The key teachings of Amos' message in this chapter are:

- Be warned: **do not worship** at the shrines of **false gods**.

- You rich people of Israel are the ones who **despise justice**.

- For example, you exploit the poor by making them give you **grain for nothing**.

- But be warned because you won't be able to live in your **expensive houses**.

- You take **bribes in the law courts** so that the poor do not receive justice and even good people keep quiet.

- But be warned: God is coming to **judge** Israel.

- God hates your false worship, he knows your religious sacrifices and hymns mean nothing.

- So, '**Let justice roll on like a river**'.

## Key ideas

- Amos was preaching around **760 BC**.

- Under King **Jeroboam**, Israel was enjoying a time of great **peace** and **prosperity**.

- Amos' message was to **condemn** the **king** and the **people** for **failing to worship God**.

- They were **hypocrites**. They were worshipping the **Assyrian** gods and pretending to worship God.

- The **Law of Moses** was being largely **ignored** by the rich and powerful.

- **Example of injustice**: the rich **bribed** the **judges** so the poor would lose their cases.

- **Example of injustice**: landlords (rich) made their **tenants** (the poor) pay **extra rent in grain** as well as their ordinary rent payments.

- **Repentance** means to **turn back to God**, change one's attitudes, seek justice and treat the poor with respect.

- **Judgement**. God would send them into **exile** and would **reverse** their present fortunes (e.g. the rich would become poor, the free become slaves).

- Justice as a **river** symbolises the **cleansing** and purifying effects of true justice.

## Contemporary issues and evaluation

*Sample question*

**Q.** Is there anything wrong with being rich?

*Points to consider:*

**On the one hand...** some argue that it is an unjust and unreliable society which relies on some people helping the poor. The rich are unlikely to offer the poor the kind of lifestyle they lead.

**On the other hand...** others argue that there is nothing wrong with being rich but rather it is how you use your wealth. The rich are in a better position to help the poor.

*Sample question*

**Q.** Should we only buy Fair Trade products?

*Points to consider:*

**On the one hand...** some argue that we in the West are very **well off** compared to many countries and often we have more than we need. **Social justice** demands that we should have a little less so the poor should not be **exploited**.

**On the other hand...** others argue **Fair Trade** products are **more expensive** than non-Fair Trade products and therefore we will **not buy** as much. Therefore the farmers and workers will earn less. We should have the freedom to choose what we buy.

---

*Sample question*

**Q.** Should society only reward those who work hard?

*Points to consider:*

**On the one hand...** some argue that many people who work very hard earn very little because the rich control how much they get paid. For this to change the **minimum wage** should be strictly enforced.

**On the other hand...** others argue that it is not how hard you work which matters but the **importance of the job** which should be rewarded. Those who have socially very **responsible** jobs should be paid more.

---

*Sample question*

**Q.** Should religion be involved with politics?

*Points to consider:*

**On the one hand...** some argue that religion is a matter of personal belief. The Church, for example, should be concerned with worship and prayer.

**On the other hand...** others argue that religion must be involved with politics if society is unjust and failing to look after the poor and the unemployed.

 **Your turn**

Now try the sample questions above for yourself.

## 2.12 Amos the prophet

Read: *Amos 7: 10–17*

### Short questions

From the official vocabulary list, questions might be asked such as:

Q. What is a prophet?

A. Someone chosen by God to speak God's message to people.

Q. What is meant by justice?

A. Treating others fairly.

Q. What is worship?

A. Giving God praise and honour.

### Summary points of the story

Amos has received a series of powerful visions from God and delivered a message of judgement to Israel:

- **Amaziah**, the priest of Bethel, sent a message to King **Jeroboam**.

- He told the King that **Amos** was causing **trouble**.

- Amos was telling the people that the **King** would **die** and they would be sent into **exile**.

- Amaziah met Amos and told him to **go home**.

- Amos answered that he was **not a professional prophet** but a shepherd and trader.

- But Amos said that Amaziah could not stop him prophesying what **God told him to say**.

- Amos warned Amaziah that many people in Israel would **die**, the **land** would be given to others and many would be **exiled** to a foreign country.

### Key ideas

- **Amaziah** was **Jeroboam's spiritual advisor**.

- Amaziah thinks that if Amos is a **professional prophet** he should go home and rejoin his **official group**.

- Amos says that he is **not a professional** prophet and so he **does not belong** to a particular group.

- This means he can **preach** God's message **wherever** he feels he called to do so.

- Unlike the King's prophets, Amos' message does not tell the King what he would like to hear.

- Amos' message is **dangerous** because it is causing people to **doubt** the King's authority.

- His **message** is very **strong**: **repent** (change your ways) or be **judged** (your life turned upside down) by God.

## Contemporary issues and evaluation

### Sample question

**Q.** Are there any prophets today?

### Points to consider:

**On the one hand...** some think there are. There are those like **Bob Geldof** and **Oscar Romero** who are prepared to stir up governments and people to act for the poor and exploited. They do not mind becoming **unpopular**.

**On the other hand...** others think there are none. A true prophet does not belong to an **organisation** – Romero was a bishop; they should call people to **repent** – Geldof's message is not based on a belief in **God**.

### Sample question

**Q.** Was Amos a success?

### Points to consider:

**On the one hand...** some think Amos was a **success**. His message is **timeless** and has inspired many to seek justice. **Martin Luther King** quoted Amos in his speeches to help end American injustice against black people.

**On the other hand...** others think he was a **failure**. The northern kingdom was **invaded** by the Assyrians and many people exiled. They had clearly ignored Amos' message. People today ignore Amos and consider his message is too **extreme**.

### Your turn

Now try the sample questions above for yourself.

# Summary

You should now know the main points and ideas behind:

1.  The First Creation story.

2.  The Second Creation story.

3.  The nature and fall of man.

4.  The story of Cain and Abel.

5.  The near sacrifice of Isaac.

6.  The Ten Commandments.

7.  The story of David and Jonathan.

8.  The story of David, Bathsheba and Nathan's parable.

9.  Solomon's wisdom.

10. The story of Elijah and the prophets of Baal.

11. Amos' message.

12. Amos the prophet.

You should also know:

The main contemporary issues relating to each of these stories.

# Test yourself

Before moving on to the next chapter, make sure you can answer the following questions. The answers are on pages 177-179

## 1.  The Second Creation Story

(a)  Name two ways God punished Adam and Eve.                                    (2)

(b)  Describe the main features of the Garden of Eden.                           (6)

(c)  Explain what the creation story teaches about human stewardship
     of the world.                                                              (6)

(d)  'We aren't always responsible for the consequences of our actions.'
     Do you agree? Give reasons to support your answer.                         (6)

## 2. The Ten Commandments

(a) What is Sinai? (2)

(b) Outline any five of the Ten Commandments. (6)

(c) Explain what the Ten Commandments teach about the relationship between God and humans. (6)

(d) 'The aim of any punishment is to make the wrong-doer suffer.'
Do you agree? Give reasons to support your answer. (6)

## 3. David and Bathsheba

(a) What is temptation? (2)

(b) Describe how David came to marry to Bathsheba. (6)

(c) Explain what this story teaches about David as a ruler. (6)

(d) 'Leaders should be punished more if they misuse their authority.'
Do you agree? Give reasons to support your answer. (6)

## 4. Amos' message

(a) What is meant by justice? (2)

(b) Describe Amos' message of judgement on Israel. (6)

(c) Explain Amos' teaching on justice and repentance. (6)

(d) 'We should only buy Fair Trade products.' Do you agree?
Give reasons to support your answer. (6)

# Chapter 3: New Testament texts and contemporary issues

There are twenty texts in this chapter, which may be tested in Section 2 of the examination paper. Have a copy of the Bible to hand and read the relevant verses noted at the beginning of each section.

## 3.1 The temptations of Jesus

Read: *Luke 4: 1–13*

### Short questions

From the official vocabulary list, questions might be asked such as:

Q.   What is temptation?

A.   The desire to do something wrong.

Q.   What is worship?

A.   Giving God praise and honour.

Q.   What is fasting?

A.   Going without food to make a person more aware of God.

Q.   What is meant by the term Son of God?

A.   Jesus' unique relationship with God.

### Summary points of the story

- After his baptism Jesus was led to the **desert** by the **Spirit**.

- The **devil** tempted Jesus for **40 days**.

- He **ate nothing** for 40 days.

- The **devil tempted** him in three ways:

    1.   The devil told Jesus that if he was the Son of God he could turn **stones** into **bread**.

         Jesus answered that **man does not live on bread alone**.

    2.   The devil led him to a **high place** and offered him all the **kingdoms of the world** if he would **worship** him.

         Jesus answered that **only God** should be **worshipped**.

    3.   The devil led him to **Jerusalem** and to **a high place** and told him that if he **jumped off** God's angels would catch him.

         Jesus answered that you must not **test** God.

- The **devil left him** and **angels** looked after him.

## Key ideas

- **Baptism**. John the Baptist's water baptism symbolised the cleansing of people's hearts and being prepared for the coming of God's kingdom. But for Jesus it also marked the moment when he felt God's very special **calling** by the **Holy Spirit**.

- **Ate nothing**. Jesus' fast is a **test of his obedience** to God and to become clearer what his mission is as God's **Son**.

- **The desert** is a reminder of **Moses'** and the Israelites' time wandering in the **wilderness for 40 years**. Moses and the Israelites were often tempted to abandon God during this time.

- **Stones into bread**. Unlike Adam in the Garden of Eden, Jesus resists selfishly eating during his time of fasting. This shows his **obedience** to God.

- **Man does not live…** The Israelites were obedient to God because God sent manna from heaven, but true obedience comes from listening to God's word.

- **Kingdoms of the world**. Moses was offered Canaan by God but here the devil offers Jesus the whole world. As **messiah** Jesus could have had **huge political power**.

- Jesus' reply that **only God should be worshipped** suggests that only desiring worldly power is a form of **idolatry**. This is clearly forbidden in the Ten Commandments.

- The **high place** in Jerusalem is probably a tower in the Temple. This temptation is not a physical test but a test to prove his special powers as God's messiah. In the wilderness the Israelites asked God for many miracle signs but Jesus shows that true belief in God's love does **not require external signs**.

## Contemporary issues and evaluation

*Sample question*

**Q.** Does power always corrupt those in positions of responsibility?

*Points to consider:*

**On the one hand…** some argue that power does corrupt because all people are **weak-willed** and power is exciting. The example of the Fall illustrates that humans are flawed and struggle to be good.

**On the other hand…** others argue there are some exceptional people who do keep to their promises and beliefs. **Jackie Pullinger** chose to help the outcasts in Hong Kong not for power or fame but because she felt it was her **vocation**.

> ### Sample question
>
> **Q.** Should one always obey God?
>
> ### Points to consider:
>
> **On the one hand...** some argue that in theory the statement is true. If God is all powerful then what he commands must **always be for the good**. However, sometimes it takes a great deal of prayer and reflection to be certain it is God's call and not our own **selfish temptations**.
>
> **On the other hand...** others argue that this is a **dangerous view** because it is not always clear what God is commanding. Some terrorists think they are carrying out God's commands when clearly God would not ask anyone to kill innocent people.

> ### Sample question
>
> **Q.** Is cheating wrong if no one finds out and no one is hurt by it?
>
> ### Points to consider:
>
> **On the one hand...** some think that there are some moral values which are **always wrong**. Cheating makes you less reliable, it may hurt others **indirectly**, it is a basic cause of injustice.
>
> **On the other hand...** others argue that if no one is hurt then the **ends justify the means**. It is impossible to claim that there are some things which are always and absolutely wrong, so cheating is wrong only if it upsets others.

 **Your turn**

Now try the sample questions above for yourself.

# 3.2 Jesus and Zacchaeus

Read: *Luke: 19: 1–10*

## Short questions

From the official vocabulary list, questions might be asked such as:

Q. What is meant by salvation?

A. Being saved and brought into relationship with God.

Q. What is meant by Son of Man?

A. Jesus' role as the one who would suffer for others.

Q. What is meant by sacrifice?

A. Giving up something for something of greater value.

## Summary points of the story

- Jesus was passing through **Jericho**.

- **Zacchaeus** was the **chief tax collector** and very wealthy.

- He **climbed** a sycamore **tree** to see Jesus better because he was **short**.

- When **Jesus** came to the tree he told him to **come down**.

- Jesus wanted to **stay at his house** straight away.

- The **crowd** was **annoyed** that Jesus should want to stay with a 'sinner'.

- Zacchaeus immediately said he would give **half his possessions to the poor**.

- He would also **pay** all those **he had cheated four times** the amount he had stolen.

- Jesus said that Zacchaeus had received **salvation**.

- Jesus said, 'The **Son of Man** came to seek and save what was lost'.

## Key ideas

- **Tax collectors** in Jesus' time were mistrusted because they worked for the Romans and often overtaxed people so they could become rich.

- **Sinners** refers to all those **excluded** from the **Jewish Law** and therefore shunned by religious people.

- **Jericho** was a **major tax point** for people entering Palestine from the east.

- Zacchaeus as chief tax collector was very rich because he had a share **in all the taxes** coming into Jericho.

- Zacchaeus' **conscience** leads him to make a big effort to see Jesus and listen to his teaching.

- Zacchaeus **repents** because he knows what he has done is wrong, **not because he wants social recognition**.

- Staying with a sinner must have **shocked** the religious people of Jericho because it would have made Jesus **religiously unclean**.

- Jesus calls himself the **Son of Man** because his role is to **represent all people to God** and prepare them for the Kingdom of God.

## Contemporary issues and evaluation

---

### Sample question

**Q.** Do we have a duty to help outcasts today?

### Points to consider:

**On the one hand...** some argue that often people are lonely, depressed or lose their jobs and therefore turn to drink, drugs and prostitution which can result in prison. Organisations such as the **Salvation Army** help them because the same situation could happen to us and because all humans are equally important and equally valued.

**On the other hand...** others think that often people **create their own problems** through greed or weakness. We **do not have a duty** to help them and we should help those who are genuinely ill, old or disabled.

---

### Sample question

**Q.** Did Jesus set a bad example by staying with Zacchaeus?

### Points to consider:

**On the one hand...** some think that Jesus did set a bad example because it is wrong to mix with people who **have low moral standards** and might even be dangerous.

**On the other hand...** others think that Jesus judged that Zacchaeus wanted help and **he took a risk**. Helping those rejected by society can be dangerous. **Jackie Pullinger's** work in Hong Kong with drug users, etc. required a lot of courage and conviction and is a good example of **moral behaviour**.

---

 **Your turn**

Now try the sample questions above for yourself.

# 3.3 Jesus and Levi

Read: *Mark 2: 13—17*

## Short questions

From the official vocabulary list, questions might be asked such as:

Q. What is meant by disciple?

A. Follower or student.

Q. What is meant by sin?

A. Disobeying God and being separated from Him.

## Summary points of the story

- **Jesus** was walking by the **sea of Galilee**.

- He saw **Levi** the **tax collector**.

- Jesus said, '**Follow me**' and Levi followed.

- **Jesus** was having **dinner** with **Levi**, other '**sinners**' and his **disciples**.

- The **Pharisees** criticised him.

- Jesus replied that it is not the **healthy who need a doctor but the sick**.

- He had come to **call sinners** not the righteous.

## Key ideas

- **Tax collectors** in Jesus' time were mistrusted because they worked for the Romans and often overtaxed people so they could become rich.

- Levi was probably **rich,** although not as well off as Zacchaeus.

- Jesus **calls Levi** with the **same** simple **words** as he called his first **disciples**.

- Levi **immediately** follows or becomes a disciple.

- **Sinners** refers to all those **excluded from the Jewish Law** and therefore shunned by religious people.

- Eating with a sinner **shocked** the Pharisees because it would have made Jesus religiously **unclean**.

- Jesus **puns** on the idea of being a **doctor** because 'doctor' also means **saviour,** one who can heal sins.

- The **sick** therefore are **sinners** and **Jesus'** role is to remove the sins which **block their relationship with God**.

- In **Matthew's Gospel Levi is called Matthew**, so it is **possible** after Jesus' death he **wrote** down a lot of Jesus' teachings.

## Contemporary issues and evaluation

*Sample question*

**Q.** Did Jesus set a bad example by having a meal with Levi?

*Points to consider:*

**On the one hand...** some think that Jesus did set a bad example because it is wrong to mix with people who **have low moral standards** and might even be dangerous.

**On the other hand...** others think that Jesus judged that Levi wanted help and **he took a risk** by showing that God sides with sinners. This is typical of the way Jesus befriended outcasts to show that God especially welcomed sinners. Helping those rejected by society can be dangerous. **Jackie Pullinger's** work in Hong Kong with drug users etc. required a lot of courage and conviction and is a good example of **moral behaviour**.

*Sample question*

**Q.** Do we have a duty to help outcasts today?

*Points to consider:*

**On the one hand...** some argue that often people are lonely, depressed or lose their jobs and therefore turn to drink, drugs and prostitution which can result in prison. Organisations such as the **Salvation Army** help them because the same situation could happen to us and because all humans are equally important and equally valued.

**On the other hand...** others think that often people create their own problems through greed or weakness. We **do not have a duty** to help them and we should help those who are **genuinely** ill, old or disabled.

 **Your turn**

Now try the sample questions above for yourself.

# 3.4 Jesus, the woman and Simon the Pharisee

Read: *Luke 7: 36–50*

## Short questions

From the official vocabulary list, questions might be asked such as:

Q.  What is a parable?

A.  Story or saying comparing the Kingdom of God with everyday human events.

Q.  What is sin?

A.  Disobeying God and being separated from Him.

Q.  What does salvation mean?

A.  Being saved and brought into relationship with God.

## Summary points of the story

- **Jesus** was having dinner with a rich **Pharisee called Simon**.
  - A **sinful woman** brought a jar of perfume.
  - As she **wept** she washed Jesus' **feet with her tears**.
  - She dried his feet with her **hair** and put **perfume** on them.
  - **Simon was amazed**. He thought that if Jesus was a prophet he would know she was a sinner.
- Jesus told Simon a parable about a money lender and **two debtors**.
  - In the parable one owed **500 denarii** and the other **50 denarii**.
  - The money lender **cancelled both debts**.
- Jesus asked Simon which of the **debtors** would **love** the money lender more.
- Simon answered the **one who had the bigger debt**.
- Jesus said that **Simon had failed** to act as the woman had.
- Simon had not given him a kiss, washed his feet and put perfume on them or anointed his head.
- The woman's many sins had been forgiven because **she loved much**.
- Her faith had **saved** her.

## Key ideas

- The contrast is between **Simon** who carries out his **minimum duties** as a host and the **woman's extravagant devotion** and **love**.

- The **Pharisees** were a group of **religious Jews** (but not priests) who thought you could only be good if you kept to all the laws of the Torah (Jewish Law).

- As a **sinful woman** she was probably a **prostitute** and therefore unable to carry out the Law.

- The story teaches about **prejudices**. The woman is stereotyped as a bad person, although there is no evidence to suggest this is true.

- It was **traditional to wash** and anoint a **guest** if he had travelled during the heat of the day.

- The **parable of the two debtors** is a reminder of Jesus' teaching in the **Lord's Prayer** to 'forgive us our debts' (trespasses) as 'we **forgive** those who are **in debt to us**'.

- **Debt** can mean literally those who **owe us money** but also those who have **sinned**.

## Contemporary issues and evaluation

*Sample question*

**Q.** Can racism be solved by better education?

*Points to consider:*

**On the one hand...** some think that equal opportunities are not enough because people **stereotype** racial minorities without any evidence. Education is a way of making sure decisions are based on knowledge not **prejudice**.

**On the other hand...** others think that far more important than education is making sure that there is **a strict equal opportunities policy** for jobs, allowances and schools. Prejudice is caused when there is bias towards one group more than another.

**Your turn**

Now try the sample questions above for yourself.

# 3.5 The call of the disciples

Read: *Luke 5: 1–11*

## Short questions

From the official vocabulary list, questions might be asked such as:

Q.  What is a disciple?

A.  Follower or student.

Q.  What is a miracle?

A.  Act of God which breaks the laws of physics.

Q.  What is sin?

A.  Disobeying God and being separated from Him.

Q.  What is faith?

A.  Having an active trust in someone or in God.

## Summary points of the story

- **Jesus** was **teaching** a crowd by the **Sea of Galilee**.

- He got into **Simon Peter's boat** and asked him to row out.

- He taught the **people from the boat**.

- Then he told Simon Peter to go into the **deep waters** and put down his **nets**.

- **Simon Peter** said they had **caught nothing so far**.

- He did as Jesus said and caught a **huge amount of fish**.

- The other fishermen rowed out and also filled their boat with fish.

- Simon Peter fell at Jesus' feet and said that he was **not worthy of Jesus** because he was a **sinner**.

- Jesus told him **not to be afraid**.

- He said that from now on they were to '**catch men**'.

- The fishermen **left everything** and followed Jesus.

## Key ideas

- The story makes a **contrast** between the **faith of the large crowds** and **Peter's lack of faith**.

- The catch of the large number of fish is a **symbol** of the **large number of followers Jesus has**.

- Filling the boat full is a **symbol** that the **Kingdom of God brings fulfilment** and abundant joy.

- **Peter's confession** to Jesus shows that he **understands** the **symbol** of the catch of fish and that he is **not worthy of the Kingdom of God**.

- Peter's **humility** is just what is needed to make him a **good disciple**.

- The disciples are to **transfer** their skills as fishermen to become **disciples** and **preach**.

- Leaving their nets shows the **sacrifice** needed to become a disciple.

## Contemporary issues and evaluation

---

### Sample question

**Q.** Does having faith in God mean one should never doubt his existence?

### Points to consider:

**On the one hand...** some argue that doubt implies a **lack of faith**. If a person doubts God's existence then they are **not a true follower**. Faith in God does not require proof of his existence.

**On the other hand...** others argue that doubt is a sign that a person realises that they **cannot know everything**. Peter's humbleness in front of Jesus was a way of showing that faith also means having to trust in things we do not always fully understand.

---

### Sample question

**Q.** Is loving one's family more important than loving God?

### Points to consider:

**On the one hand...** some argue that religion can sometimes break up families and this can never be right. Christianity teaches the **importance of marriage and duties** to parents so it could never be the case that the love of God means leaving one's family.

**On the other hand...** others argue that Jesus never taught that a person should not love their family but should be clear what their **ultimate values** are. As **God is all powerful** and all loving then there may be times when loving God must be more important.

---

 **Your turn**

Now try the sample questions above for yourself.

# 3.6 The rich young man

Read: *Mark 10: 17–31*

## Short questions

From the official vocabulary list, questions might be asked such as:

Q.  What is a disciple?

A.  Follower or student.

Q.  What is justice?

A.  Treating others fairly.

Q.  What does sacrifice mean?

A.  Giving up something for something of greater value.

Q.  What is a parable?

A.  Story or saying comparing the Kingdom of God with everyday human events.

## Summary points of the story

- The man asked Jesus what he should do to **inherit eternal life**.
    - **Jesus** told him to keep the **Ten Commandments**.
    - The man said he had **kept** these since he was a child.
    - Jesus challenged him to **sell everything** and give it to the poor.
    - The man was **sad and left**. He was very rich.

- **Jesus** said to the **disciples** that **rich people** would find it **hard** to get a place in the **Kingdom of God**.

- The disciples were **amazed**.

- Jesus told them a **parable**: it would be easier for a **camel to pass through the eye** of a needle than a rich man to enter the **Kingdom of God**.

- Peter said they had left everything to follow Jesus.

- Jesus replied everyone who had left his family and property would **receive it back a hundred times over** in **the Kingdom of God**.

## Key ideas

- In the 1st century having **great wealth** was a sign that you had been **blessed** by God.

- The **man** just **wants Jesus to praise him** for keeping the Ten Commandments and being a good person.

- But Jesus' challenge is to **reverse** the man's religious views and ask him to **give to the poor**.

- As **God sides with the poor** the man is being challenged to see whether he really believes in **justice**.

- Jesus' **disciples clearly also fail to understand** the nature of justice.

- Jesus imposes a **tough choice on his followers**: their primary aim should be to fulfil the demands of the Kingdom of God – that might mean **leaving one's family**.

- The **reward** in the Kingdom of God is **justice** and **spiritual fulfilment**.

- The parable Jesus tells illustrates an **impossible problem**; a camel cannot fit through the eye of a needle.

## Contemporary issues and evaluation

### Sample question

**Q.** Does the love of money cause injustice?

### Points to consider:

**On the one hand...** some argue that there are many examples where the love of riches has meant that the **poor have suffered great injustices**. **Mother Teresa** in India and **Oscar Romero** in Latin America both worked to fight against injustice caused by the rich failing to distribute their wealth.

**On the other hand...** others argue that although this could be true, it is only by **having money** that it is then possible to **help the poor** and help overcome injustice. If there was no love of money people would not **work hard** to acquire it.

### Sample question

**Q.** Is loving one's family more important than loving God?

### Points to consider:

**On the one hand...** some argue that religion can sometimes break up families and this can never be right. Christianity teaches the **importance of marriage and duties** to parents so it could never be the case that the love of God means leaving one's family.

**On the other hand...** others argue that Jesus never taught that a person should not love their family but to be clear what their **ultimate values** are. As **God is all powerful** and all loving then there may be times when loving God must be more important.

*Your turn*

Now try the sample questions on the previous page for yourself.

# 3.7 The request of James and John

Read: *Mark 10: 35–45*

## Short questions

From the official vocabulary list, questions might be asked such as:

Q.  What does the phrase the Son of Man mean?

A.  Jesus' role as the one who would suffer for others.

Q.  What is baptism?

A.  Symbolic washing away of sin.

Q.  What is atonement?

A.  Getting back into a right relationship with God.

## Summary points of the story

- **James** and **John** asked whether they could sit at Jesus' **right and left hand side** in the Kingdom of God.

- Jesus said they had not really understood what this would mean.

- He asked them whether they could '**drink the cup**' he drinks or be '**baptised with the baptism**' he was baptised with.

- They said they could.

- Jesus told them that they would undergo his **baptism**.

- But he **could not tell** them where they would be **placed** in the **Kingdom of God**.

- The other **disciples were annoyed** when they heard about James' and John's request.

- Jesus told them not to **squabble** about **having authority**.

- They were all to become **servants to each other** because as **Son of Man** he had come **to serve** and to be a '**ransom for many**'.

## Key ideas

- **James and John have misunderstood** Jesus' teaching about the Kingdom of God. They think it will be a **political kingdom**.

- James and John ask to **have key political roles** in the Kingdom of God.

- Jesus also refers to **drinking the cup** at Gethsemane where it refers to his role as the **suffering** servant who will **die for others**.

- Jesus implies that **James and John** will also **suffer** and die as **martyrs** and disciples.

- Being **baptised** means being **called by God** to follow Jesus and being prepared to **die** for one's beliefs.

- In the Kingdom of God there will be **no rulers** because all followers will **serve the needs** of others.

- A **ransom** is the price paid to free a slave (or a hostage). Jesus says his death will **pay for our sins** so that in the **Kingdom of God** we will be free.

## Contemporary issues and evaluation

### Sample question

**Q.** Should a Christian be prepared to die for others?

### Points to consider:

**On the one hand...** some argue that in following Jesus' example it is better to **sacrifice** one's self for the good of others than let evil win. **Oscar Romero** knew that fighting for the rights of the poor of Latin America might lead to his assassination, and it did.

**On the other hand...** others argue that it is not always clear when dying is **sacrificial** or **suicidal**. Sometimes people have offered to die for others because it makes them look **heroic**. Christian teaching regards **suicide** as selfish and **sinful**.

### Sample question

**Q.** Should religion be kept separate from politics?

### Points to consider:

**On the one hand...** some argue that religion is about developing a **personal and spiritual relationship with God**. Jesus' teaching on the Kingdom was about repentance and forgiveness of sin not about running the country.

**On the other hand...** others argue that religion is about **changing society** in accordance with God's will. That means protecting the weak and removing social sins. The Old Testament prophets fearlessly gave God's message to the rulers of their day, and Jesus' teaching on the **Kingdom looked for a transformation of society**. Thus religion has to be involved with politics, as **Bonhoeffer** argued when he was involved in the plot to kill Hitler.

Now try the sample questions on the previous page for yourself.

# 3.8 The paralysed man

Read: *Mark 2: 1–12*

## Short questions

From the official vocabulary list, questions might be asked such as:

Q. What is a miracle?

A. Act of God which breaks the laws of physics.

Q. What is sin?

A. Disobeying God and being separated from Him.

Q. What is faith?

A. Having an active trust in someone or in God.

Q. What does the phrase Son of Man mean?

A. Jesus' role as the one who would suffer for others.

Q. What is blasphemy?

A. Speaking against God or making oneself equal to God.

## Summary points of the story

- **Jesus** was at **Capernaum**.

- There were **so many people that four men** who carried a **paralysed man** could not get near Jesus.

- So they climbed onto the **roof** of the house, dug a hole in it and **lowered the man down**.

- When Jesus saw their **faith,** he said to the paralysed man that his **sins were forgiven**.

- But the **lawyers** present **criticised** Jesus and said his words were **blasphemy** – only **God can forgive sins**.

- Jesus said to them that forgiving sins and healing amounted to the same thing.

- But anyway the **Son of Man** had **authority** to forgive sins.

- Jesus told the man to **pick up his mat** and go home.

- Everyone was **amazed**.

## Key ideas

- In the 1st century some **illnesses** were considered to be punishment by God for **sin**.

- Jesus cures the paralysed man because of the **faith** of the four **friends**.

- **Blasphemy** is when a person sets themselves up to be equal with God.

- Jesus is accused by the lawyers of blasphemy. The **punishment for blasphemy** in Jewish law could be the **death penalty**.

- Jesus' answer is to show his concern for the man's **body** and **soul**.

- The people are **amazed** because the **lawyers** cannot **think of a reply** to Jesus' words.

## Contemporary issues and evaluation

*Sample question*

**Q.** Do healing miracles happen today?

*Points to consider:*

**On the one hand...** some argue that God can and does work in ways which we do not understand. There are many reported healings at **Lourdes** which doctors cannot explain.

**On the other hand...** others think there are better ways of explaining unusual cures. The **mind** can sometimes give people **unusual inner strength**. In many cases 'cures' turn out to be short term and it is clear there has been no miracle.

*Sample question*

**Q.** Is it right to help someone to die?

*Points to consider:*

**On the one hand...** some argue that it is right to help someone who is dying by **relieving the pain** but never right to shorten their lives by killing them. This is the view of **Cicily Saunders**. She set up the **hospice** movement to give the dying a dignified death.

**On the other hand...** others think that it is **cruel** to make someone go through a lot of pain and it would be more caring and loving to end their lives when **they want it** with their family around them.

Now try the sample questions on the previous page for yourself.

# 3.9 Jesus heals a crippled woman on the Sabbath

Read: *Luke 13: 10–17*

## Short questions

From the official vocabulary list, questions might be asked such as:

Q.  What is a miracle?

A.  Act of God which breaks the laws of physics.

Q.  What is the Sabbath?

A.  Jewish day of rest.

## Summary points of the story

- **Jesus** was **teaching** in a synagogue on the **Sabbath**.

- A **woman** who had been **crippled for 18 years** was in the congregation.

- **Jesus** put his hands on her and said she would be '**set free**' from her illness.

- The synagogue leader said Jesus had **broken the law** by working on the Sabbath.

- Jesus said they were **hypocrites**.

- The law allowed them to **feed their animals** on the Sabbath.

- So should he not be allowed to cure this woman on the Sabbath?

- Jesus' **critics** were **humiliated** by his argument.

- But the **people were delighted** with Jesus.

## Key ideas

- In the 1st century some **illnesses** were considered to be punishment by God for **sin**.

- **Jesus 'frees'** her from her illness and the **sin** which had caused it.

- According to the Jewish law it was **illegal to work by healing on the Sabbath**.

- The **Jewish law** did allow someone to **save a life** on the Sabbath.

- Jesus' argument shows how **hypocritical** the **religious leaders** were by valuing their animals' lives more than a human being.

- Jesus' action shows his **compassion** for the sick.

## Contemporary issues and evaluation

*Sample question*

**Q.** Should euthanasia be legal?

*Points to consider:*

**On the one hand...** some argue that it is wrong to have a law which stops people offering a merciful death as an option. We **do not let animals suffer** so we should not let people suffer. The **law** should just **protect people** from making hasty decisions.

**On the other hand...** others argue that if the law allows euthanasia people might **not feel safe** going to **hospital** if the doctors have the option of killing their patients. As there are **hospices** such as **Helen House** which give a great deal of support to very ill children and their families, then there is no need to make euthanasia legal.

*Sample question*

**Q.** Was Jesus actually able miraculously to cure the sick?

*Points to consider:*

**On the one hand...** some argue that **Jesus** clearly had a **gift** to cure the sick and people recognised this as a gift from God. **Miracles** can be defined as a moment when **God is felt** to be involved in a special way. Jesus' healings helped to reinforce his teaching about the reality of **the Kingdom of God**.

**On the other hand...** others argue that there is a great deal more that **we understand about the mind** today than in Jesus' time. Jesus may have had a great gift of helping others to overcome their difficulties but it is **unlikely** that he **actually did the impossible**. Some stories are probably **exaggerated**.

 *Your turn*

Now try the sample questions above for yourself.

# 3.10 Peter's declaration

Read: *Mark 8: 27–33*

## Short questions

From the official vocabulary list, questions might be asked such as:

Q.  What does the term Son of Man mean?

A.  Jesus' role as the one who would suffer for others.

Q.  What does messiah or Christ mean?

A.  The anointed one.

Q.  What is a prophet?

A.  Someone chosen by God to speak God's message to people.

## Summary points of the story

- **Jesus** and his **disciples** were near **Caesarea Philippi**.

- Jesus asked the **disciples** who the people **thought he was**.

- They **answered** that some thought he was **John the Baptist**.

- Some thought he was **Elijah**.

- Some thought he was a **prophet**.

- Jesus asked the disciples who they thought he was.

- **Peter** said that Jesus was the **messiah**.

- Jesus told them not to tell anyone this.

- **Jesus** said that as the **Son of Man** he would **suffer**.

- He would be **rejected** by the **Jewish authorities**.

- But he would **rise again** after **3 days**.

- **Peter** told Jesus that he would **not let him do this**.

- But **Jesus** told **Peter not to tempt him**.

- Jesus said to him '**Get behind me Satan**'.

- **Peter** was thinking in **human terms** and not as God wished.

## Key ideas

- There were many **Jewish ideas** about who the **messiah** would be, but everyone imagined the messiah would bring a time of **peace, compassion** and **justice**.

- **Ordinary people** thought Jesus was **very special. John the Baptist** had been killed shortly after Jesus' baptism and some thought his spirit was now living on in Jesus.

- **Elijah** was the great Jewish **prophet** in the Old Testament and some hoped he would bring back **true worship of God**. Some think his spirit is living on in Jesus.

- **Peter** believes Jesus is the **messiah** whose healings and teachings are bringing the time of peace and compassion.

- Jesus explains that he also sees his **role as messiah** as one who will **suffer for others**.

- Peter's reaction suggests he **cannot believe** that a **messiah** will **suffer**.

## Contemporary issues and evaluation

*Sample question*

**Q.** Was Jesus just a good man?

*Points to consider:*

**On the one hand...** some argue that the evidence supports this view because Jesus did not encourage the use of force or violence and he taught to **love** one's enemies and **help the weak**. His **miracles** and his **resurrection** are just exaggerated stories or **myths** to make him appear very special.

**On the other hand...** others argue that Jesus was a good man but he was also the messiah and **Son of God**. There is no reason to make up his **miracles** or the **resurrection** and these could only happen if God was working in Jesus in **some very special way**.

**Your turn**

Now try the sample questions above for yourself.

# 3.11 The transfiguration

Read: *Mark 9: 2–13*

## Short questions

From the official vocabulary list, questions might be asked such as:

Q. What does the word transfiguration mean?

A. Change of appearance.

## Summary points of the story

- **Jesus** took **Peter, James** and **John** up a **high mountain**.

- **Jesus** was **transfigured**.

- His **clothes** were **dazzling white**.

- **Elijah** and **Moses** appeared **talking** to Jesus.

- **Peter** suggested that they **build three shelters** for Moses, Elijah and Jesus.

- A **cloud** appeared and from it a **voice** spoke.

- 'This is my **Son** whom I love. **Listen** to him'.

- Suddenly Moses and Elijah had gone and only Jesus was there.

- On the way down **Jesus** told the **disciples not to tell anyone** what they had seen.

- The disciples asked Jesus why **Elijah** must first come.

- Jesus explained that **Elijah** must come first to **restore society**.

- In fact he had come.

- So now Jesus, as the **Son of Man**, would **suffer** many things.

## Key ideas

- The **transfiguration** reveals to the disciples Jesus' **divine identity** as God's son.

- Transfiguration means to **change appearance**.

- The event describes the **disciples' spiritual experience** of who Jesus is.

- In their **vision** the disciples see Moses and Elijah: **Moses** represents the **law** and **Elijah** represents Jewish **prophecy**.

- **Jesus** is **greater** than these two figures and therefore is the **fulfilment** of the **law** and the **hope of the prophets**.

- It was believed that **Elijah** would come to prepare the people for the messiah. So, if **John the Baptist fulfils Elijah's** role then **Jesus is the messiah**.

## Contemporary issues and evaluation

 *Your turn*

Now try the sample questions above for yourself.

# 3.12 The Good Samaritan

Read: *Luke 10: 25–37*

## Short questions

From the official vocabulary list, questions might be asked such as:

Q. What is a parable?

A. Story or saying comparing the Kingdom of God with everyday human events.

## Summary points of the story

• A **lawyer** asked Jesus, 'Teacher, what must I do to **inherit eternal life?**'.

• **Jesus** asked him what the **law** said.

• The lawyer answered that he should **love God** and **love his neighbour** as himself.

• The lawyer asked Jesus, '**Who is my neighbour?**'

- Jesus answered with a parable:
  - A man was travelling from **Jerusalem** to **Jericho**.
  - Robbers **beat** him up and left him for **dead**.
  - A **priest** saw the man and **crossed** to the other side of the road.
  - A **Levite** saw the man and **crossed** to the other side of the road.
  - A **Samaritan** took **pity** on him, fed him and bandaged his wounds.
  - He took him to an **inn** and gave **the innkeeper money** for further care of the man.
- Jesus asked the lawyer who was the **neighbour** to the man.
- The lawyer answered the one who had **mercy** on him.
- Jesus told him to go and **act** in the same way.

## Key ideas

- The **traditional Jewish** answer to the question 'Who is my neighbour?' would be '**other Jews**'.

- The point of the parable illustrates the **prejudices** people have about who is worthy to be considered a neighbour.

- In Jewish law a **dead body** and blood were considered **religiously unclean**.

- The **priest** was probably on his way to the Temple and could not touch the body otherwise he would not have been allowed into the Temple.

- A **Levite** is an assistant in the Temple, like the priest he would not be allowed to touch a dead body.

- **Neither men made any effort** to find out whether the man was dead or not.

- The **Samaritans** were **despised** by the Jews and treated as racially and socially inferior.

- The Samaritan acts **generously, mercifully** and out of **love**. He fulfils the essence of the Jewish law.

## Contemporary issues and evaluation

### Sample question

**Q.** Is racism the worst form of prejudice?

### Points to consider:

**On the one hand...** some argue that racism is the worst form of **prejudice** because racism has caused terrible **wars** and **massacres** such as the slaughter of the Tutsi by the Hutu in **Rwanda**. Racism also causes **mistrust** and **discrimination** in local communities based on false views of other people.

**On the other hand...** others argue that other forms of prejudice such as **sexism** can be just as destructive for society. Women make up half the world's population but still they find themselves **underpaid** by comparison with men. Women often fail to get the top jobs and are **not taken as seriously** as men.

### Sample question

**Q.** Were Jesus' parables the best way to teach?

### Points to consider:

**On the one hand...** some argue that we **remember stories** much better than straight teaching. Jesus' parables were able to use events from everyday life to **explain complex ideas about the Kingdom of God** very effectively.

**On the other hand...** others argue that however good Jesus' parables were, his **most important teaching** was done **without parables**. Sometimes parables can **confuse** or people **do not understand their hidden message**.

 **Your turn**

Now try the sample questions above for yourself.

## 3.13  The Lost Son

Read: *Luke 15: 11–32*

### Short questions

From the official vocabulary list, questions might be asked such as:

Q.  What is a parable?

A.  Story or saying comparing the Kingdom of God with everyday human events.

Q.  What is sin?

A.  Disobeying God and being separated from Him.

### Summary points of the story

- A man had **two sons**.

- The **younger son** asked whether he could **have his inheritance now**.

- The younger son set off to a distant land and **spent everything** having a good time.

- When **famine** struck he went to work looking after **pigs**.

- He was extremely **hungry**.

- He realised his father's servants were in a better state than himself.

- He decided to **return home**.

- He would say to his father '**I have sinned against heaven and against you**'.

- While he was some way off his **father saw him** and rushed to meet him.

- His father told the servants to put a **ring on his finger**, kill the fatted calf and prepare a **feast**.

- He said that they should rejoice that his **dead son was now alive**, '**He was lost and is found**'.

- But the **elder son** was **angry** and told his father that he had never been given a party like this.

- His father answered that the elder son had **continually enjoyed** everything he owned.

- But today it was appropriate to **celebrate** the **return** of the son who was lost and now is found.

## Key ideas

- The parable is aimed at the **Pharisees** who were critical of Jesus' concern for outcasts.

- This parable is one a series about the '**lost**' people of Israel, that is those who were considered to be sinners, those rejected by the Jewish law.

- In the parable the **elder son** represents the **Pharisees** or all those who have kept to the law but are unable to be generous to those who have fallen short of its demands.

- The **younger son** represents **outcasts and sinners** of society.

- **Eating with pigs** is an important idea in the parable. As pigs were considered unclean in the Jewish law the younger son has reached an emotional and religious low.

- The younger son's **return** illustrates the need for all humans to **repent,** i.e. the realisation of one's faults.

- The **father** represents how **God's redemption**, that is his generosity, love and forgiveness is for all sinners.

- The **feast** symbolises **joy** in the Kingdom of God.

## Contemporary issues and evaluation

*Sample question*

**Q.** Were Jesus' parables the best way to teach?

*Points to consider:*

**On the one hand...** some argue that we **remember stories** much better than straight teaching. Jesus' parables were able to use events from everyday life to **explain complex ideas about the Kingdom of God** very effectively.

**On the other hand...** others argue that however good Jesus' parables were, his **most important teaching** was done **without parables**. Sometimes parables can **confuse** or people **do not understand their hidden message**.

**Your turn**

Now try the sample questions above for yourself.

## 3.14 The Sower

Read: *Luke 8: 4–8, 11–15*

### Short questions

From the official vocabulary list, questions might be asked such as:

Q. What is a parable?

A. Story or saying comparing the Kingdom of God with everyday human events.

### Summary points of the story

Jesus told the crowd this parable:

- A farmer sowed his **seed**.
- Some seed fell on the **path**.
- It was **trampled** on and eaten by **birds**.
- Some fell on **rock**.
- It **died** because it had **no moisture**.
- Some fell amongst **thorns**.
- It **grew** a little but was then **choked**.
- Some fell on **good soil**.

- This seed yielded up **100 times** more seed than was sown.

Jesus explained the parable to his disciples:

- The **seed** is the **Word of God**.

- The seed on the **path** is like people who **do not believe** because the **devil** makes them **disbelieve**.

- The seed on the **rock** is like people who **receive** the word with **joy** but they have **no stamina** and when life gets difficult they **give up**.

- The seed amongst the **thorns** is like people who after a while find **life's cares** and **desire for money choking** their faith.

- The seed in the **good soil** is like those who have '**good and noble hearts**'. They persevere and flourish.

## Key ideas

- The parable illustrates how **different people react** to Jesus' teaching about the Kingdom of God.

- The **Kingdom of God** is **God's presence in our lives now**, not just heaven.

- The parable teaches that the Kingdom **requires effort**; even though some people want to experience it they give up for various reasons.

- Jesus probably told the parable to **encourage** his **disciples** when they felt they had **failed** in their preaching about God's Kingdom.

## Contemporary issues and evaluation

*Sample question*

**Q.** Is the teaching of the Parable of the Sower mostly about coping with failure?

*Points to consider:*

**On the one hand...** some argue that this is true because the demands of the Kingdom of God of forgiveness, loving one's enemies, etc are great and the parable shows how most people are **unable to live up to its expectations**. The parable is teaching Christians how to cope when they fail to convert other people to Christianity.

**On the other hand...** others argue that although some people will fail to accept Christianity there are many millions who have become Christians and societies have been **transformed** by its message. Our culture, law and morality owe a great deal to Jesus' teaching. The parable is about being **optimistic**.

**Your turn**

Now try the sample questions above for yourself.

# 3.15 Jesus' teaching

Read: *Luke 6: 17–49*

## Short questions

From the official vocabulary list, questions might be asked such as:

Q.  What is justice?

A.  Treating others fairly.

Q.  What is a parable?

A.  A story or saying comparing the Kingdom of God with everyday human events.

## Summary points of the story

Jesus gave the following **sermon 'on a level place'** to his **disciples**:

**The Beatitudes**

*Blessed are:*

- those who are **poor** will **receive** the **Kingdom of God**;

- those who are **hungry** will be **satisfied**;

- those who **weep** will **laugh**;

- those who are **persecuted** because of their faith will be **blessed**.

**The Woes**

*Woe to:*

- the **rich** for they have received their **reward** now;

- the **well fed** for they will go **hungry**;

- those who **laugh** for they will **weep**;

- those who **are well thought of** for they will find out that it was **not meant**.

## Loving enemies

- Love your **enemies** and do **good** to those who hate you.

- If someone **strikes** one cheek, **offer the other** also.

- If someone **takes** your **cloak**, **offer** your **tunic**.

- **Do to others as you would have them do to you**.

- Do not just love those who love you.

- Do not just **lend** to those who you know will repay you.

- **Be merciful just as your Father is merciful**.

## Judging others

- Do not **judge** and you will not be judged.

- **Forgive** and you will be forgiven.

- Can **a blind man lead a blind** man? No they will **both fall into a hole**.

- Do not look at the **speck of dust** in your brother's eye when you have a **plank in your** own eye.

- Do not be **hypocritical**; remove the plank first and then you will be able to see clearly to remove the speck.

## Parable of the tree and its fruit

- A **good tree** does **not** bear **bad fruit**.

- A tree is recognised by its fruit.

- You do not pick **figs** from **thorn bushes**.

- So a **good person** brings out **good** things **stored in his heart**.

- A **bad person** brings out **bad** things **stored in his heart**.

**Parable of the wise and foolish builders**

- Real and false faith are like two builders.

- The **good builder** built his **foundations** on rock.

- When the **floods** came his house remained **firm**.

- But the **foolish builder** did **not lay down** foundations.

- When the **floods** came his house **collapsed**.

- He is like the man who hears my **words** but does **not put them into practice**.

## Key ideas

- **Jesus** is presented **like Moses** giving a **new law** on how to live in the Kingdom of God.

- The **blessings** describe the **right attitudes** needed to become members of the Christian community (the Kingdom of God).

- **Blessed** people are those who work to **overcome injustice** such as poverty, hunger and persecution.

- **Cursed** people are those who are **selfish**, unconcerned with justice and helping others.

- **Loving enemies**. It was traditional to hate your enemies, so Jesus' teaching poses a great **challenge** to our usual feelings.

- The word love or **agape** (in Greek) means **being more generous** than would be expected.

- **Judging others**. As **none** of us are **entirely good** we are **not** in a position to **judge others**. Only God can be the ultimate judge.

- Jesus often **criticised** those who are **hypocrites**, saying one thing but doing something else. Here he teaches that his followers **must practise what they preach**.

- The parable of the **wise and foolish builders** shows that **true faith requires effort** and long-term **commitment**.

# Contemporary issues and evaluation

## Sample question

**Q.** Is pacifism more effective than war?

### Points to consider:

**On the one hand...** some argue that **Jesus** explicitly taught we should **love our enemies**. Violence can only lead to more violence and in wars it is the innocent who often suffer. If Martin Luther King could use **non-violent protest** to defeat the evils of racism then this must be the better option.

**On the other hand...** others argue that although pacifism should be the aim of our **personal relationships** with each other, sometimes war is necessary when it comes to **protecting a large number** of people against an **evil force**.

## Sample question

**Q.** Should we always forgive those who wrong us?

### Points to consider:

**On the one hand...** some argue that if we do not forgive those who wrong us we **harm ourselves further**. The anger within us could also lead us to become **bitter** or dangerous.

**On the other hand...** others argue that there are some actions which **are so bad** that they cannot be forgiven. Furthermore forgiving some people implies that they have **done no wrong** and this might lead them to carry on doing bad things.

**Your turn**

Now try the sample questions above for yourself.

# 3.16 Crucifixion

Read: *Mark 15: 6–41*

## Short questions

From the official vocabulary list, questions might be asked such as:

Q. What is the Sanhedrin?

A. Jewish ruling council made up of seventy councillors and the High Priest.

Q. What does the term Son of God mean?

A. Jesus' unique relationship with God.

Q. What does atonement mean?

A. Getting back into a right relationship with God.

Q. What does worship mean?

A. Giving God praise and honour.

## Summary points of the story

**Jesus before Pilate**

- It was a custom at **Passover** to **release a prisoner**.

- The people wanted **Barabbas**.

- **Barabbas** was a **murderer** and had led several revolts.

- **Pilate** asked whether he should **release Jesus** 'the King of the Jews'.

- But the chief **priests** stirred up the crowd to **release Barabbas**.

- **Pilate asked** what he should do with Jesus.

- The **crowd** shouted '**Crucify him**!'.

- **Pilate** asked what **crime** Jesus had done but the crowd still shouted 'Crucify him!'.

- Pilate **released Barabbas** and had **Jesus flogged**.

## The soldiers mock Jesus

- The **soldiers** led **Jesus** to the **praetorium**.

- They dressed him in a **purple robe**.

- Put a **crown of thorns** on his head.

- They called out '**Hail King of the Jews!**'.

- The struck him and spat on him.

- They pretended to **worship** him.

- Then they put his own clothes back on and led him to be crucified.

## The Crucifixion

- The soldiers made **Simon of Cyrene** carry Jesus' cross.

- At Golgotha they offered him **drugged wine** but Jesus refused it.

- The soldiers crucified him.

- They **cast lots** for his clothes.

- The charge above Jesus' head read '**The King of the Jews**'.

- **Two robbers** were crucified with him.

- **Passers-by taunted** him by saying that if was able to knock down the Temple and rebuilt it he could also save himself from the cross.

- Members of the **Sanhedrin** mocked him saying that although he saved others he could not save himself.

## Jesus' death

- The land was plunged into **darkness**.

- In the **afternoon** Jesus cried out 'Eloi, Eloi lama sabachthani'.

- Which means 'My God, my God why have you forsaken me?'.

- Some **thought** he was **calling** for **Elijah**.

- One man offered him a **sponge with wine vinegar** on the end of a stick to drink.

- He wondered whether Elijah would save Jesus.

- Jesus **died** with a **loud cry**.

- The **curtain of the Temple** was torn in two.

- When the **centurion** saw how Jesus had died he said, '**Surely this man was the Son of God**'.

- Women who had followed from Galilee watched along with many other women from Jerusalem.

## Key ideas

- It is **not clear** why the **Jewish authorities**, the **Sanhedrin**, wanted Jesus **dead**.

- The reasons might be that **Jesus** was **popular** and they feared they might **lose their authority**.

- They thought he was **blasphemous** by making himself equal with God.

- **Pilate** and the **Roman authorities** might have thought that as Jesus claimed to be a 'king' or messiah, that this was **treason** against **Caesar** and he should die.

- **Pilate** might have been **weak-willed** and just wanted to keep the crowds quiet.

- Jesus' death is a **sacrifice** for human **sin**. As the suffering servant (the Son of Man) his death is an offering to God as a '**ransom**' to bring people back to God.

- Jesus' death is therefore an **atonement**; making humans 'at one with' God.

- The ransom is symbolised by the tearing of the **Temple curtain** in two which shows that the **barrier between God and humans** is now **removed**.

## Contemporary issues and evaluation

---

### Sample question

**Q.** Was Pilate to blame for Jesus' death?

### Points to consider:

**On the one hand...** some argue that as governor of Judea at the time he could have dismissed the Sanhedrin's charges. He could see that **Jesus was not really a king** and was no threat to the Romans. Pilate is to blame because he was **weak-willed** and should have acted fairly.

**On the other hand...** others argue that Pilate was aware that at Passover time Jerusalem was packed with pilgrims and that if he made the wrong decision he could have a bloody **riot on his hands**. He may have thought Jesus was innocent but it was more important to **keep the peace**. It was the **Sanhedrin who were to blame**.

---

### Sample question

**Q.** Was it really necessary for Jesus to die?

### Points to consider:

**On the one hand...** some argue that in an imperfect world the sacrifice of some for others makes it possible for life to carry on. This is what happened in the story of the *Miracle on the River Kwai* when a **soldier gave up his life to save hundreds of others from being executed.** Jesus' death was also a sacrifice.

**On the other hand...** others argue that Jesus did not intend to die and that his **teaching** and **healings** could easily have been **sufficient** to make his message about God's Kingdom clear. His **death** was **unfortunate** but **not necessary**.

---

### Your turn

Now try the sample questions above for yourself.

## 3.17 Burial

Read: *Mark 15: 41–47*

### Short questions

From the official vocabulary list, questions might be asked such as:

Q. What is the Sabbath?

A. Jewish day of rest.

### Summary points of the story

- It was the day when the **Sabbath** was being prepared.

- **Joseph of Arimathea**, a member of the Sanhedrin, asked Pilate for **Jesus' body**.

- **Pilate** asked the **centurion** if Jesus was **dead**.

- Joseph took Jesus' body and wrapped it in **linen**.

- He placed the body in a **tomb** in a **cave**.

- **Mary Magdalene** and **Mary** the mother of Jesus **saw** where he was **laid**.

### Key ideas

- The burial takes place **quickly** on Friday afternoon **before the Sabbath. The Jewish Sabbath** rules mean that no work can be done, which includes a burial.

- **Joseph of Arimathea's** presence shows that **not all** the **Sanhedrin condemned** Jesus.

- As an influential member of society he is able to provide a tomb for Jesus' body.

- The presence of the **women** is as **witnesses** that Jesus' body was **actually buried** and **not stolen**.

## Contemporary issues and evaluation

### Sample question

**Q.** Do the women show greater faith in Jesus than his male disciples?

### Points to consider:

**On the one hand...** some argue that as **Peter denied** Jesus and **Judas betrayed** him and the **others had fled** then it is true that they did not show complete faith in Jesus. The **women** had **followed** Jesus from Galilee and without fuss had **supported** him right up to his burial.

**On the other hand...** others argue that the **disciples** had more **risky roles**. No one would have taken much notice of the women but the men might easily have been **imprisoned or killed on the same charges as Jesus.** Their loss of faith was only brief – they came to Jesus' tomb later before the women.

 **Your turn**

Now try the sample questions above for yourself.

## 3.18  The resurrection

Read: *John 20: 1–29*

### Short questions

From the official vocabulary list, questions might be asked such as:

Q.  What does resurrection mean?

A.  Rising to new life from the dead.

Q.  What does the term Son of God mean?

A.  Jesus' unique relationship with God.

### Summary points of the story

**The empty tomb**

- Very **early** on the first day of the week **Mary Magdalene** came to Jesus' tomb.

- She saw the **stone** had been **moved** and ran to tell **Peter** and the **Beloved Disciple**.

- Peter and the Beloved Disciple **came** to the tomb.

- When Peter looked in he saw the **linen cloths** lying there **neatly**.

- The Beloved Disciple arrived and looked in and **believed**.

## Mary Magdalene and Jesus

- **Mary Magdalene** stood by the tomb **weeping**.

- She saw **two angels** in the tomb standing at the head and feet of where Jesus had lain.

- They **asked** her why she was weeping.

- She said because they had taken her **Lord away**.

- She turned round and **saw Jesus** but **did not recognise** him.

- He **asked** her why she was weeping.

- As she thought he was the **gardener**, she asked him where the body had been put.

- He said '**Mary**'.

- She said '**Rabboni**' and tried to **hold** him.

- Jesus told her **not to touch** him because he had not yet returned to his Father.

- **Mary returned** to the **disciples** to tell them that she had **seen the Lord**.

## Jesus appears to his disciples

- On the **first day of the week** Jesus appeared to the **disciples**.

- They were **eating** a meal **behind locked doors**.

- Jesus said to them '**peace be with you**'.

- He showed them the **marks** of the **crucifixion**.

- Jesus said he was **sending them to preach**.

- He **breathed** on them as a sign of the **giving** of the **Holy Spirit**.

- He gave them **authority to forgive sins**.

## Jesus appears to Thomas

- **Thomas** had not been with the disciples.

- He said he would **not believe** unless he had seen Jesus' marks of crucifixion.

- A week later Jesus **passed through** the **locked doors**.

- He told Thomas to put his **finger in the marks on his hands and side**.

- Thomas said '**My Lord and my God**'.

- Jesus said that those who **believed without seeing were also blessed**.

- Jesus continued to **perform more miracles**.

## Key ideas

- **Resurrection** means that after Jesus' death he was brought back to life, not as a ghost but in some kind of **spiritual body**.

- The resurrection is **experienced** in very **different** ways by each set of people in the story.

- **Women** have a **key role** in the resurrection story. This shows the revolutionary teaching of Jesus because in Judaism women could not become disciples or teach.

- **Peter and the Beloved Disciple** believe in the resurrection based on the **absence** of Jesus' body.

- But **Mary Magdalene** is the **first** to 'see' the resurrected Jesus. She may **not have recognised him** because she **was not expecting to see him** or because he **was not physically the same**.

- Mary Magdalene had led a sinful life before meeting Jesus early on in his ministry.

- Mary Magdalene is told **not to touch Jesus** because she has to **learn** to **believe** in the resurrection without having the physical presence of Jesus to depend on.

- The story of **Thomas** teaches that Jesus **was not a ghost** and that belief has to be based on **experiencing God's love** not physical proof.

- Jesus **breathes on the disciples** as a sign that the **Holy Spirit will continue his work** in their hearts.

- **Luke** describes the coming of the Holy Spirit at **Pentecost** in a slightly different way in Acts 2 (the disciples experience a great wind and tongues of fire). But the meaning is the same.

## Contemporary issues and evaluation

 ### *Your turn*

Now try the sample questions above for yourself.

# 3.19 Events of Pentecost

Read: *Acts 2: 22–24, 40–41*

## Short questions

From the official vocabulary list, questions might be asked such as:

Q. What is baptism?

A. Symbolic washing away of sin.

Q. What is a miracle?

A. Act of God which breaks the laws of physics.

Q. What is crucifixion?

A. Roman death penalty of being nailed to a cross.

Q. What is salvation?

A. Being saved and brought into relationship with God.

Q. What is resurrection?

A. Rising to new life from the dead.

## Summary points of the story

After the Holy Spirit had descended on the Apostles and enabled them to speak in all the languages of the crowds, Peter gave a speech:

- **Jesus** of Nazareth was **sent by God** as he was able to perform many **miracles** and signs.

- **God handed** him across to **wicked** people who **crucified** him.

- But **God raised** him from the dead and **freed** him from death.

- **Peter warned** them to **save** themselves from the **corruption** of society.

- About **3000 believed** and were **baptised**.

## Key ideas

- **Pentecost** was a major **Jewish festival** in Jerusalem. It would have been attended by Jews from **all** over the **civilised world**.

- The **Holy Spirit** was described as descending on the Apostles like **fire and wind**, both **symbols** of **God's presence**.

- The **Holy Spirit** enabled the Apostles to **speak** in all the **various languages** of the **Jews present**. This **symbolised** the **arrival** of the **Kingdom of God** and how the effects of the **Tower of Babel** had been reversed.

- In the **Old Testament** the **Tower of Babel** was when God **punished** the people for trying to be greater than God. The punishment was that they would speak different languages and not understand each other.

- **Peter's** speech explains how **Jesus' death** was the reason why God sent his **Holy Spirit**.

- **Pentecost** is **traditionally** thought of as the **birth of the Christian Church**.

## Contemporary issues and evaluation

*Sample question*

**Q.** Do different languages divide the world more than anything else?

*Points to consider:*

**On the one hand...** some argue that language is part of **culture** and lack of understanding of another person's language can cause **misunderstanding** and **mistrust**.

**On the other hand...** others argue that although languages can cause problems what really divides the world and causes conflict is the **uneven distribution of wealth**.

*Sample question*

**Q.** Should there be divisions in the Christian Church?

*Points to consider:*

**On the one hand...** some argue that Jesus did **not intend** there to be **divisions** within the Church because he **criticised** his disciples for looking for **personal power** when they **should** have been **working together**.

**On the other hand...** others argue that as Jesus was **tolerant** of many types of people so the different Church traditions should allow different forms of worship, even different ways of **interpreting Christian teaching**.

 *Your turn*

Now try the sample questions above for yourself.

# 3.20 How the early Christians lived

Read: Acts 2: 42–47

## Short questions

From the official vocabulary list, questions might be asked such as:

Q. What does worship mean?

A. Giving God praise and honour.

Q. What is a miracle?

A. Act of God which breaks the laws of physics.

## Summary points of the story

- The early Christians met and **studied** the **teaching of the Apostles**.

- They **broke bread** together and **prayed** and worshipped God.

- Many **miracles** and signs were **performed** by the **Apostles**.

- They **shared everything**.

- They **sold** all their possessions.

- They gave to the **poor**.

- They met every day in the **courts of the Temple**.

## Key ideas

- The idea of **Church** is not a building but the **gathering of Christians**.

- The early Church practised a form of **communism**.

- Everyone is **equal**.

- Everyone must be **provided for**.

- The 'breaking of bread' is both an **ordinary meal** but probably also a **holy communion** which shows how important **worship** was in their community life.

## Contemporary issues and evaluation

---

### Sample question

**Q.** Should the Church get back to her roots and give up all its wealth?

### Points to consider:

**On the one hand...** some argue that wealth has **corrupted** the purpose of the Church. Many Christians are more concerned with **status and promotion** within the Church than they are in prayer and helping the oppressed and the weak.

**On the other hand...** others argue that it was **easy** for the very **early Christians** to live simple lives without great wealth but the Church today is like any other **organisation** and **needs wealth** in order to operate and provide help and assistance to those who need it.

---

### Sample question

**Q.** Should there be divisions in the Christian Church?

### Points to consider:

**On the one hand...** some argue that Jesus did not intend there to be **divisions** within the Church because he **criticised** his **disciples** for looking for **personal power** when they should have been **working together**.

**On the other hand...** others argue that as Jesus was **tolerant** of many types of people so the different Church traditions should allow different forms of worship, even different ways of **interpreting Christian teaching**.

---

 **Your turn**

Now try the sample questions above for yourself.

## 3.21 The Apostles are persecuted

Read: *Acts 5: 17–42*

### Short questions

From the official vocabulary list, questions might be asked such as:

Q. What is the Sanhedrin?

A. Jewish ruling council made up of seventy councillors and the High Priest.

Q. What is resurrection?

A. Rising to new life from the dead.

## Summary points of the story

- The **high priest arrested** the **Apostles** and put them in jail.

- But an **angel opened** the **prison** doors.

- And told them to go to the **Temple** courts to **teach**.

- The **chief priest** sent the **Sanhedrin** to **fetch** the Apostles from jail.

- But although they **found** the prison **doors locked**, the **Apostles had gone**.

- Then someone saw the Apostles in the Temple teaching.

- The **captain of the guard** brought the Apostles to the Sanhedrin.

- The high priest told them that he had **forbidden** them to **teach**.

- **Peter** answered, '**We must obey God rather than men!**'.

- He went on to say that Jesus' death and resurrection by God was to bring **repentance** and **forgiveness**.

- The **Sanhedrin** wanted to **kill them**.

- But the **lawyer Gamaliel** said that **Theudas** and **Judas** had both **claimed** to be **messiahs** and led revolts but **nothing** had come of it.

- He **advised** them to **let the Apostles go**.

- If their teaching was from God then there would be **nothing they could do** to stop them because they would be fighting against God.

- The **Sanhedrin agreed** with **Gamaliel**.

- The **Apostles** were **flogged** and **continued teaching** in the Temple courts.

## Key ideas

- In the **Sermon on the Plain** Jesus had **taught** that his **followers would be persecuted** and be blessed as a result.

- The **Apostles** were following in Jesus' footsteps and **upset** the **Jewish authorities**, the **Sanhedrin**.

- The Apostles are punished both for **preaching blasphemy**, i.e. claiming that Jesus is the Son of God and **causing a public nuisance** in the Temple courts.

- However, not every one regarded the Apostles' message as **dangerous** and **Gamaliel's** solution was **quite a reasonable one**.

# Contemporary issues and evaluation

---

## Sample question

**Q.** Should Christians only side with the oppressed?

### Points to consider:

**On the one hand...** some argue that an important part of **Jesus' message** was to **fight** against **injustice** and although this can be dangerous, it is working to give all people dignity. **Jackie Pullinger's** work with the poor in Hong Kong was a result of her Christian calling.

**On the other hand...** others argue that if Christians only side with the oppressed it is **too extreme** and there are many others who, though not oppressed, equally need helping in their everyday lives just by **being good neighbours**.

---

## Sample question

**Q.** Should a person question their beliefs?

### Points to consider:

**On the one hand...** some argue that when a person's beliefs are leading them or others into **dangerous situations** then it is quite right to wonder whether these beliefs are sound. No belief should cause another **person's death**, for example.

**On the other hand...** others argue that a real test of a person's beliefs is in an extreme situation. **Testing** one's belief is **different from questioning it**. For example **Bonhoeffer** tested his commitment as a Christian when he became involved in the plot to kill Hitler and to be a traitor to his country.

---

 **Your turn**

Now try the sample questions above for yourself.

# Summary

You should now know the main points and ideas behind the following:

1. The temptations of Jesus.

2. The story of Jesus and Zacchaeus.

3. The story of Jesus and Levi.

4. The story of Jesus, the woman and Simon the Pharisee.

5. The call of the disciples.

6. The story of the rich young man.

7. The request of James and John.

8. The healing of the paralysed man.

9. The story of Jesus healing a crippled woman on the Sabbath.

10. Peter's declaration.

11. The transfiguration.

12. The parable of the Good Samaritan.

13. The parable of the Lost Son.

14. The parable of the Sower.

15. Jesus' teaching.

16. Jesus' crucifixion.

17. Jesus' burial.

18. The resurrection.

19. The events of the Pentecost.

20. The account of how the early Christians lived.

21. The account of how the Apostles were persecuted.

You should also know the main contemporary issues relating to each of these stories.

# Test yourself

Before moving on to the next chapter, make sure you can answer the following questions. The answers are on pages 180-182.

## 1. On being a follower of Jesus: the rich young man

(a) What does sacrifice mean? (2)

(b) Outline the story of the rich young man. (6)

(c) Explain what this story teaches about wealth and discipleship. (6)

(d) 'No one should have great wealth.' Do you agree? Give reasons to support your answer. (6)

## 2. Who was Jesus? Peter's declaration

(a) What does the title Son of Man mean? (2)

(b) Describe the conversation between Jesus and his disciples at Caesarea Philippi. (6)

(c) Explain what this event teaches about Jesus' role as the Messiah. (6)

(d) 'Jesus was no more than just a good man.' Do you agree? Give reasons to support your answer. (6)

## 3. Parables: the sower

(a) What is the meaning of the term parable? (2)

(b) Outline the parable of the Sower. (6)

(c) Explain why Jesus told this parable. (6)

(d) 'Most people do not have strong beliefs.' Do you agree? Give reasons to support your answer. (6)

## 4. The early Christians: how the early Christians lived

(a) What does worship mean? (2)

(b) Describe how the early Christians lived. (6)

(c) Explain the key beliefs of the early Christians. (6)

(d) 'Christians should not disagree with each other.' Do you agree? Give reasons to support your answer. (6)

# Chapter 4: World religions: Christianity

Chapters 4–9 cover Section 3 of the examination. You only need to revise a minimum of one world religion for the examination. If you are not sure which one to revise, then check with your teacher.

**BC** means **Before Christ**.

**AD** means **Anno Domini** or the 'the year of our lord', i.e. the year when Jesus was born.

The western dating system is based on Christianity. However, you will see below that most scholars date Jesus' actual birth to be earlier than the year 1.

These revision notes follow the order of Kevin O'Donnell's *The Christian Experience*. You must make sure that you understand and learn the ideas in *The Christian Experience* as well as the notes below.

Use these ideas and the notes below to build up your knowledge and create your own system to remember them. (See *Study Skills* by Elizabeth Holtom, published by Galore Park, for ideas on creating mind maps to assist you.)

## 4.1 Jesus

Jesus is the central figure of Christianity.

- Jesus was born in **Bethlehem** around **4 BC**.

- Not much is known of his early life in **Nazareth**.

- At the age of 30 he was **baptised by John the Baptist** and felt that God had **specially chosen him**.

- He lived, worked and **preached** around **Galilee**.

- He chose **12 men** as his **disciples**.

- He performed **miracles** especially **healings**.

- He **taught** about **preparing** for the **Kingdom of God**.

- His **parables** explained how **love** is more important than **keeping to religious laws**.

- His teaching often **upset** the **Jewish** and **Roman authorities**.

- He was **betrayed by Judas**, one of his disciples, **to the Jewish authorities**.

- The **Jewish** authorities **handed him over** to the **Romans**.

- Pontius **Pilate**, the Roman Governor, sentenced him to **death**.

- He was **crucified** in 29 AD.

- **Three days later** he **rose** from the dead.

- He **ascended** into **heaven** to be with God.

- Christians believe he is the **Son of God** and the **Risen Lord**.

- Christians believe his death **pays off** people's **sins**.

# 4.2 Church denominations

The Christian Church is divided into many groups called **denominations**. These are formed depending on their members' differing interpretations of Christianity. A denomination therefore refers to a group of Christians who have particular teaching and worship which they think are important.

## The East/West split

In the 11th century AD a major split occurred between Christians in the West (the Catholic church) and those in the East (the Orthodox church) which has still not been healed.

- The first major **split** in the Church happened in **1054 AD**.

- It was caused by an **argument** about who should **lead the church**.

- Those in the **Eastern** churches became known as the **Orthodox church**.

- The **centre** of the Eastern churches was **Constantinople**.

- Those in the **West** were known as **Catholics** (later called Roman Catholics).

- The **centre** of the Catholic church was **Rome**.

- The **leader** of the Catholic church was known as the **Pope**.

## Main denominations

Some denominations only have a few thousand followers. Others, like the Roman Catholic Church, have millions worldwide.

- There are **300 Christian denominations** throughout the world today.

- The **Orthodox** Church comprises the Greek Orthodox and Russian Orthodox churches.

- The **Roman Catholic** Church has millions of people throughout the world.

- The **senior bishop** of the Roman Catholic Church is the **Pope**. He resides in the **Vatican**.

- The **Protestant** churches emerged in the **15th century** during the **reformation** when they **rejected** the **authority** of the **Catholic** church.

- Examples of the protestant churches today are Lutheran, Baptist, United Reformed and Pentecostal churches.

- The **Anglican Church** was created when **Henry VIII** became **head of the church in England** and not the Pope.

- Today the Anglican Church can be found throughout the world. There are many 'churches' within it such as the Church of England, the Episcopal Church of Scotland, the Episcopalian church in the USA, etc.

- The **Archbishop of Canterbury** is the **senior** bishop of the **Anglican** churches.

- The **ecumenical movement** is a modern movement working to bring different Church traditions **together**.

- The ecumenical **symbol** is a **cross in a boat on the sea**.

# 4.3 Bible

The Bible contains the central beliefs of the Christian faith and followers are encouraged to read it.

## The Bible

- The term **bible** means **many books**.

- The **Old Testament** contains the **Jewish scriptures** such as law, prophets, history and poetry.

- The **New Testament** contains the four Gospels, Acts of the Apostles, many letters and the book of Revelation.

- The **Gospels** tell of **Jesus' life**, teaching, death and resurrection.

- The term **gospel** means **good news**.

## The authority of the Bible

Some Christians consider the Bible to have a great deal of authority on how they should lead their everyday lives.

- The Bible for Christians is the **Word of God**.

- The writers of the Bible were **inspired** by God's **Holy Spirit** to write it.

- The Bible contains the **code for living**.

- It contains **truth**.

### Difficulties with the Bible

The Bible contains elements that are hard to understand or can be interpreted differently.

- Some of the **violent** stories in the Old Testament **clash** with **Jesus' teaching on love**.

- There are many **miracle** stories which modern people find **difficult** to believe happened.

- It is sometimes difficult to know when a story is **symbolic** or **literal**.

- It is not always clear which **laws** of the Old Testament **Jesus rejected**.

## 4.4 Beliefs

The **main** Christian **beliefs** are contained in the **Creed**. The main points referred to in the Creed are:

### The Trinity

- There is **One God** who exists in **three persons**.

- He is **Father**, the **creator** of all things and who is beyond us.

- He is **Son** who in **human form is Jesus Christ**, who is 'God with us'.

- He is **Holy Spirit**, who is everywhere around us and the **source of inspiration**.

### The Holy Spirit

- The Holy Spirit is the **third person** of the Trinity. It:

  - lives or **dwells** on earth in the **hearts of people** and in the **Church**.

  - is **invisible**.

  - gives **comfort**.

  - inspires **prayer**.

  - is the source of **truth**.

  - is **symbolised** by **wind**, **dove**, **fire** and **water**.

  - inspired people to write the **Bible**.

## Jesus Christ

- Jesus is the **incarnation** of the **Son,** the **second person** of the **Trinity**.

- **Incarnation** means to **become human**.

- Jesus died for the **sins of the world**.

- His **resurrection** is a sign of **victory over sin and death**.

- He **ascended** to God the Father in **heaven**.

- Jesus' **death** and **resurrection** promises **eternal life** for believers.

- Jesus will **return at judgement day** to judge the living and those who have died.

## Sin and forgiveness

- **Sin** is **hurting** someone, yourself or God by rejecting or ignoring them.

- All people sin.

- Sin can be **deliberate** or **unintentional**.

- As God is **love** he wishes to **forgive** us our sins.

- God sent his Son to express his **love** for the world.

- Jesus died on the **cross** for our sins so that people can be **forgiven**.

- Christians should follow Jesus' example and **forgive** others.

## Life everlasting

- God will **judge** all people according to their **lives on earth**.

- God will grant **life everlasting** or **life after death** to the **faithful**.

- In **heaven** the soul of the departed can **meet** with the **souls** of **family** and **friends**.

- **Heaven** is beyond time and space.

- **Heaven** is a **mystery**.

- Heaven is **spiritual**.

- Heaven is **eternal**.

# 4.5 Baptism

Baptism is a special ceremony of welcoming somebody into the Church community. It is most often performed when the person is still an **infant**, though for some denominations it should occur when they join the Church at a later age. This is called a **believer's baptism**.

## Infant baptism ceremony

- An **infant** is baptised using a **font** filled with **water**.

- **Parents** and **godparents** make **promises** to bring up the child in a Christian way.

- The child is given a **Christian name**.

- **Water** is poured over the child's **head**.

- The **priest** prays that the child be **protected from evil**.

- The **sign of the cross** is made.

- In **Orthodox** churches the **sign is made with oil**. This is called **Chrismation**.

- A **lighted candle** is given to **parents** and **godparents** to remind them of their **duties** to the child.

## Believer's baptism

- This usually happens for people who are **12 years and older**.

- They must **ask** for it to happen.

- They must **repent** of their sins.

- They give a '**witness**' to the congregation explaining why they wish to be a Christian.

- They **repent** of their sins.

- The **minister** holds their **head** and **hand**.

- They are **plunged** backwards fully into **water**.

## Symbols used at baptism

- Baptism is the moment when a **person becomes a Christian**.

- Jesus used **water baptism** to symbolise the **end** of one's **old life** and the **beginning** of a **new** one.

- **Water** is a symbol of **life** and of **washing away sins**.

- **Oil** is a symbol of God's **Spirit**.

- The **candle** is a symbol of the **presence of Christ**, who is the light of the world.

- The **candle** also symbolises how a person passes from **darkness to light**.

## 4.6 Prayer

Christians pray for their own benefit or on behalf of other people.

### How Christians might pray

- They might go to **church** to pray and worship.

- They may use **icons** or a picture of a saint, Jesus, the Holy Family.

- They might light a **candle**.

- They might **kneel** as a sign of **humility** before of God.

- They might make the **sign of the cross**.

- They might pray to their own particular **saint**.

- They might use the **Lord's Prayer**, the prayer Jesus taught.

### Types of prayer

- Prayers which **praise** God.

- Prayers which **thank** God.

- Prayers which ask **forgiveness**.

- Prayers which ask for help or guidance for **yourself**.

- Prayers which ask help or guidance for **others** called **intercessions**.

## 4.7 Places of worship

The place of Christian worship is often at the heart of a community. It is not just a place to worship but also a place to meet people and to give or receive help.

### Typical Anglican or Roman Catholic church

- The **altar** is at the **east** end of the **church**. A **crucifix** or **cross** is placed on it to symbolise Jesus' **death and sacrifice**.

- The **pews** or seats are in the **nave** of the church for the **congregation**.

- The **pulpit** is a raised reading desk in the **nave** for **sermons**.

- The **lectern** is a reading desk used for **reading the Bible**.

- The **font** is usually at the **west** end of the church and used for **baptisms**.

- The **windows** depict **stories** from the Bible.

- An **organ** is used for music.

- There may be **side chapels** dedicated to a particular **saint**.

## Typical Baptist or Methodist church

- There is usually a **raised pulpit** in the **centre** of the building for **preaching** and **reading the Bible**.

- The **table** or **Lord's Table**, is in **front** of the **pulpit** and used for **communion**.

- There is **simple decoration**.

- Churches tend to **avoid pictures** in windows, etc.

- There are chairs/pews for people.

- There is sometimes an **organ** used for music.

## Typical Orthodox church

- There are many **icons** or special paintings of Christ and the saints.

- The main feature is an **iconostasis**, a screen containing the icons.

- The church is lit with many **candles**.

- The **font** is usually at the **west** end of the church and used for **baptisms**.

- Often there are **no pews** or seats for people, people stand.

# 4.8 Holy Communion

Holy Communion remembers **Jesus' last supper** with his disciples. When giving Holy Communion, the minister carries out the actions of Jesus in distributing bread and wine. Today the usual features in Holy Communion or the Lord's Supper are:

- **Hymns**/songs are sung at the start and throughout.

- There are **prayers** of **intercession**.

- Two readings from the **Bible follow**, from the **Old and New Testaments**.

- The minister gives a **sermon**.

- **Roman Catholics** and **Anglicans** come to the **altar rail**.

- The **priest** gives worshippers **bread and wine**.

- **Orthodox priests** come to the people and give them **bread/wine** on a **spoon**.

- In the **Free Churches** congregations drink wine in **small glasses** where they are **sitting**.

- **Bread** is **passed round**.

- **After communion** there are final **prayers** and the **blessing** given by the **priest** or **minister**.

# 4.9 Ministers

The minister or Christian leader presides over church services as well as looking after the spiritual lives of his or her community of Christians.

- An **ordained minister** is a person who has a **vocation** to be a **leader** in their church.

- A minister has also been specially **trained**.

- Different churches have different names and roles for their ministers.

- The term **minister** is used by the **Methodist** church.

- The term **pastor** is used by the **Baptist** church.

- The term **priest** is used by the **Anglican**, **Roman Catholic** and **Orthodox** churches.

- The term **bishop** refers to a **senior priest** in the **Anglican**, **Roman Catholic** and **Orthodox** churches.

- The terms **rector** or **vicar** refers to an **Anglican priest** who is in charge of a particular parish or parishes.

## Role of ministers

The minister is responsible for **organising** and **leading worship**.

The minister might:

- **Lead Bible study**.

- Help in the local **school**.

- **Visit** the **sick** in his parish.

- Organise the **Sunday school**.

- **Help the bereaved** and take **funerals**.

- **Prepare** couples for **marriage** and take **weddings**.

- **Preach** in church and **hold classes** on Christian teaching.

- **Prepare** people for **confirmation** or baptism.

- Hear **confession**.

## Arguments for and against having women ministers

Certain people have argued that women should be able to become ministers as well as men. Make sure that you understand the arguments 'for' and 'against'.

- Some Christians argue that Jesus **treated men and women equally**.

- Some Christians argue that Jesus had **many women amongst his followers**.

- Some Christians argue that he only chose male disciples because it would have been **too radical in those days** to have women disciples.

- Some Christians argue that only a **male** priest can **represent Christ** who was a **man**.

- Some Christians argue that **Jesus only chose male disciples** to be his ministers.

- Some Christians argue that men should be in charge of the church and that women's role should be to **look after the family**.

# 4.10 Marriage

Marriage plays an important part in Christian life and is an outward sign of love which was central to Jesus' teaching.

- The minister explains the **purpose of marriage**.

- Marriage is to **one person** for the **whole of this life**.

- Marriage is for **children** to **grow up securely**.

- Marriage is for two people to **grow** in **love** and **companionship**.

- The bride and groom both make **three promises** to the **congregation**:

  - They promise to **love** and be **faithful** only to each other for life.

  - They promise to **honour** each other for life.

  - They promise to **protect** and look after each other for life.

- The **minister pronounces** them to be **husband and wife**.

- **Marriage symbols** might include: the **exchange of rings**, **wearing of crowns**, wearing a **white dress**, wearing a **veil**.

- **Divorce** is only accepted in **some churches** where the **relationship has ended**.

- **Roman Catholics** do **not permit divorce** but only **annulment**, which means that the marriage is considered **never to have happened**.

# 4.11 Easter

Easter is the most important festival in the Christian year. In Holy Week Christians remember the last few days of Jesus' life and death on the cross. On Easter day there is a joyful celebration of his resurrection.

## Holy Week – Palm Sunday

- On **Palm Sunday** Christians remember **Jesus' entry** into **Jerusalem**.
- **Palm branches** are placed in churches and some wear palm crosses.
- There are church **processions** and special **services** in church.

## Holy Week – Maundy Thursday

- On **Maundy Thursday** Christians remember **Jesus' Last Supper** with his disciples.
- **Maundy** means **commandment**, when Jesus commanded his disciples to **love one another as equals**.
- As Jesus washed his disciples' feet, many **ministers wash** the **feet** of their **congregation**.
- There are special **services** of **Holy Communion**.
- Many churches hold **special prayer services**.

## Holy Week – Good Friday

- On **Good Friday** Christians remember Jesus' **trials** and **death** by **crucifixion**.
- Some churches have special **services** when all the **items on the altar** are **removed**.
- **Pictures** and **crosses** in the church are **covered** with **dark materials**.

## Holy Week – Holy Saturday vigil

- After sunset on **Holy Saturday** Christians remember the moment when **Jesus** was **raised from the tomb**.
- Worshippers wait up **late** and **pray**.
- Many light **candles** and **bonfires**.
- **Light** symbolises the **hope over evil** which the resurrection brings.

## Easter Sunday

- On **Easter Sunday** Christians remember the moment when the **women** came to the **empty tomb**.
- People attend church for special **services**.

- The **readings** in church recall when **Mary Magdalene** and the other disciples **met** the **risen Jesus**.

- There are **joyful hymns** celebrating Jesus' **resurrection**.

- People **greet** each other with '**He is risen, Hallelujah**'.

- The church is filled with **flowers** and **eggs** are given to children as symbols of **new life**.

## 4.12 Festivals

### Christmas

- **Advent** is the period of the **4 weeks preparing** for Christmas.

- People make **Advent wreaths** with four candles which they light each Sunday before Christmas.

- Some people have **Advent calendars** which mark the days up to Christmas Eve.

- On **Christmas day** Christians remember Jesus' **birth** and the **incarnation** of God in Christ.

- People **attend church** and listen to **readings** about Jesus' special **birth** in **Bethlehem**.

- **Prayers** remember the **poor**, the **sick** and **children in need**.

- It is a time of **giving to charities**.

- At home **presents** are exchanged.

### Pentecost

- At **Pentecost** (also known as Whitsun) Christians remember the **coming** of the **Holy Spirit** on the **Apostles** after **Jesus' ascension** into heaven.

- The **Apostles** were able speak in **different languages** and could be **understood** by all different nationalities.

- It is traditionally a time when people are **baptised** and become members of the Church.

- Pentecost is considered to be the **birth of the Church**.

## Harvest

- **Harvest** festival is a time of **thanking God** for **creation** and the gifts of nature.

- People bring **food** to church.

- A special **harvest loaf** is baked.

- **Hymns** remember God as **creator** and **provider**.

- The **food** is **distributed** to the **poor** in the parish.

- It is a time of giving to **charities**.

# 4.13 Pilgrimage

Pilgrimage is the act of making a journey to a place that has a special relevance to a religious belief. People who make them are known as **pilgrims**.

## Canterbury

- **Canterbury** is the **home** to the senior bishop or **archbishop** in the **Church of England**.

- **The archbishop of Canterbury** is also the senior bishop of the **Anglican** church.

- **St Thomas Becket** was martyred (killed for his belief) in Canterbury on 29th December **1170 AD**.

- **Becket** is remembered as a **saintly man** who **refused** to carry out the **orders** of **King Henry II**.

- **Miracles** were recorded at **his tomb**.

- **Canterbury** has been a very popular **pilgrimage** centre ever since.

- For example, **Chaucer's** Canterbury Tales contains the kind of **stories pilgrims told** on their way to Canterbury.

## Walsingham

- Lady **Richeldis** had a vision of **Mary** in **1061 AD**.

- In the **vision** she saw a **spring of water** which could **heal**.

- The spring was **discovered** and a special **house** was **built** over it.

- The shrine was **destroyed** in **1538 AD** but **rebuilt** in the **20th century**.

- People **today** go to seek **healing** and **peace**.

- In addition to the **Anglican** church there are **Roman Catholic** and **Orthodox** churches.

## Rome/Vatican

- The **Vatican** is **home** of the **Pope**.

- The Pope is the **successor** of **St Peter**.

- **St Peter** is **buried** beneath **St Peter's Church** in the Vatican.

- **Pilgrims** often attend large **audiences** given by the **Pope**.

- Pilgrims also **visit** other churches in Rome such as the **Basilica of St Paul**.

- They also go to the **catacombs** where **early Christians worshipped** and were **buried**.

## Holy Land

- Pilgrims visit **Bethlehem** at the Church of the Nativity where **Jesus** was **born**.

- They travel to **Galilee** and visit Capernaum where **Jesus taught**.

- Pilgrims go to the **Mount of Beatitudes** where Jesus gave the **Sermon on the Mount**.

- In **Jerusalem** they follow the **route** Jesus took to his **crucifixion** called the **Via Dolorosa**.

- Pilgrims visit **Jesus' tomb** and **pray** at the **Church of the Holy Sepulchre**.

## Lourdes

- In **1858** a young Roman Catholic girl **Bernadette** had visions of **Mary**.

- In her visions Mary pointed to a **spring of water** which could **heal**.

- A **spring** later appeared in a cave.

- Thousands come each year for the **healing gifts** of the water.

# Summary

You should now know the following:

1. The key facts about Jesus and his life.

2. The different Christian Church denominations and how these came about.

3. The importance of the Bible.

4. The main Christian beliefs outlined in the Creed.

5. The significance of baptism and the different ceremonies.

6. Types of prayer and different ways of praying.

7. How places of worship differ depending on the denomination.

8. How the Holy Communion is celebrated.

9. The types and roles of Christian ministers.

10. The role of marriage in Christian life.

11. The main acts of worship during Holy Week and the festival of Easter.

12. The main Christian festivals.

13. The main pilgrimage sites and their significance.

# Test yourself

Before moving on to the next chapter, make sure you can answer the following questions. The answers are on pages 182-183.

1. Describe the main events of Jesus' life. (5)

2. Describe what happens at a typical Christian wedding ceremony. (5)

3. Explain why the Bible is important for Christians. (5)

4. Explain what Christians believe about God. (5)

5. Describe **one** place where Christians go on pilgrimage. (5)

# Chapter 5: World religions: Judaism

You only need to revise a minimum of one world religion for the examination. If you are not sure which one to revise, then check with your teacher.

> **BCE** means **Before the Common Era** and is equivalent to using BC.
>
> **CE** means the **Common Era** and is equivalent to using AD.
>
> In traditional Judaism dates are given from the creation of the world.

These revision notes follow the order of Liz Aylett and Kevin O'Donnell *The Jewish Experience*. You must make sure that you understand and learn the ideas in *The Jewish Experience* as well as the notes below.

Use ideas from *Study Skills* by Elizabeth Holtom, published by Galore Park, to help you remember these notes and ideas.

## 5.1 Origins

You will be expected to know the following points about the origins and history of Judaism:

- **Abraham** lived around **1800 BCE** and is called the '**Father of the Jews**'.
- He lived as a **nomad** in **Ur** in **Mesopotamia** and **at first worshipped many gods**.
- However he **felt** the **call** of the **one God**.
- **God** told Abraham to **travel** from **Ur to Canaan**.
- God made a **covenant** with Abraham and promised him **land** and **many descendents**.
- Although Abraham and Sarah could not have children, **God enabled Sarah** to give birth to **Isaac**.
- God **tested Abraham's** faith by telling him to **sacrifice** Isaac.
- Abraham's **faith** was **sound** and God **renewed the covenant**.
- **Isaac** and then **Jacob** became the next **patriarchs**.
- **God changed Jacob's name** to **Israel**, the people were therefore known as **Israelites**.
- **Moses** was born in **Egypt** around **1270 BCE**.
- **Moses** tried to **persuade Pharaoh** to **free** the **Hebrew** slaves.
- **Pharaoh** was **reluctant** so **God** sent **10 plagues** and the **Hebrews escaped** through the Red Sea.

- This event is called the **Exodus**.

- In the **Exodus** to the promised land God gave **Moses** the **Torah or Law**.

- After **Moses' death Joshua** took over, **captured Jericho** and the people **settled** in **Canaan**.

- The people were then **formed** into **12 tribes**.

## 5.2 Holy books

The three terms, **Tenach**, **Torah** and **Talmud**, refer to different Jewish holy books. The **Tenach** is the whole of the Hebrew Bible (which Christians refer to as the Old Testament), of which the **Written Torah** or **Law** is part. The **Talmud** is a separate book and contains the Oral Torah.

### Tenach

- The **Tenach** refers to the whole of the **Hebrew Bible**.

- It contains the **Torah** or **Law**.

- It contains **Nevi'im** or the **Prophets**.

- Some of the great **prophets** were **Elijah**, **Nathan**, **Isaiah**, **Ezekiel** and **Jeremiah**.

- The **Tenach** contains **Ketuvim** or the **Writings**.

- Examples of the **Writings** are the **Psalms** and **Proverbs**.

### Torah

- Torah means **teaching** and contains the **written laws**.

- The **Written Torah** forms the heart of modern Jewish life.

- It is the **first five books** of the **Tenach** or Hebrew Bible.

- Torah contains **commandments** and **stories**.

- Torah is the **heart** of the **covenant** made with **Moses**.

- It contains **613 commandments** or **mitzvoth**.

- The **Ten Commandments** are the 10 central mitzvoth.

- Torah is **read** in the **synagogue**.

- The Torah scroll or **Sefer Torah** is treated with great **respect**.

- In the synagogue the Torah scroll is **read** using a **special pointer**.

## Talmud

- **Talmud** means **study**.

- It contains **stories** and **teachings** of the **rabbis** on how to **keep Torah**.

- It also contains the **Oral Torah** given to **Moses** at the same time as the **Written Torah**.

## 5.3 Beliefs

### God

- Jews believe that **God is one**, there are **no other gods**.

- God **created** the **world**.

- God **sees** and **knows everything**.

- **God** gave the **Torah** so **humans** are able to **worship Him** and **live life fully**.

- The **Shema** is the most **important** Jewish **prayer** which is said **daily**.

- The **Shema** remembers that God is one and **He alone** is to be **worshipped**.

### Messiah

- The **messiah** is God's **messenger of peace**.

- When he **arrives everyone** will **obey** the **commandments**.

- Jews are still **waiting** for his **arrival**.

- **Some** Jews think he will be an actual **person**.

- **Some** Jews think he is **not** an actual **person** but a **peaceful state of mind** in the world.

### World to come

- The world to come is called the **Olam Ha'Ba**.

- It is a future **eternal state of the world**, which will **last for ever**.

- It is **not clear** exactly what this will be like.

- **Some** think it might be an **after life** in **heaven**.

- **Some** think it might be a **life in this world** but transformed so it is **perfect**.

## 5.4 Synagogue

The synagogue is the Jewish place of worship and study but it is also used for many other community activities.

### Religious items worn by orthodox Jewish men in synagogue

- Men wear a **hat** or **kippa** as a sign of **respect** for God.
- They wear two **special prayer boxes** or **tefillin** containing the **Shema**.
- They wear a prayer **shawl** or **tallit** with **tassels** at each corner.

### Layout of a typical synagogue

- The **ark** is a **large cupboard** at the **front** of the synagogue.
- The **ark** contains the **Torah Scroll** or **Sefer Torah** and other scrolls.
- There is a **menorah** or **eight-branched candlestick**.
- The **menorah** reminds people of **God's presence**.
- In the **centre** there is a **bimah** or the raised **reading platform**.
- Men and women sit **separately** in **Orthodox synagogues**.
- **Other rooms** include schoolrooms, libraries, meeting rooms.

### Worship in the synagogue

- People must **dress modestly**. Boys and **men cover** their **heads**.
- Worship is set out in a **prayer book** called a **siddur**.
- The service is **led** by a **man or rabbi** in **Orthodox** Judaism.
- The service is **led** by any **qualified man/woman** in **Reform** Judaism.
- The service is mostly in **Hebrew** in **Orthodox** synagogues and a **mixture of Hebrew and English** in **Reform** synagogues.
- The service **begins** with the saying of several **psalms**.
- The **Sefer Torah** is **processed** from the **Ark** to the **bimah**.
- **Portions** of the **Torah** are **read** from the bimah by various people.
- The **Sefer Torah** is then **processed back to the Ark**.
- **Readings** then follow from the **prophets**.
- The **rabbi** might give a **sermon** or address.
- **Prayers** may be said for the **Royal Family**.
- The service **ends** with **Kiddush**.
- **Kiddush** is a special **blessing** made over **bread** and **wine**.

## 5.5 Orthodox and Reform Judaism

The Reform movement started in the 19th century, and quickly spread throughout the Jewish world. Some Jewish leaders felt that certain laws needed to be revised to adapt them to the modern world. Unlike Orthodox Jews members of the Reform movement do not think the Torah was given to Moses all at once, but evolved over time.

### Orthodox

- Orthodox Jews believe that **God** is the **author** of the **Torah**.
- The **Torah cannot** be **changed**.
- They believed **Moses** was also given the Oral Torah or **halakhah**.
- Men and women must **sit separately** in the synagogue.
- **Kosher laws** should be kept, e.g. milk and meat should be eaten and prepared separately.
- Women have more **laws** to fulfil at **home**.
- Men have more **laws** to fulfil in the **community**.
- Only **men** may wear **tefillin** and **tallit**.

### Reform

- Reform Jews believe that the **Torah** was written **by people** at different times.
- The **Torah** can be **adapted** for modern times.
- The **Oral Torah** or **halakhah** are **human adaptations** of the Torah.
- **Kosher food laws** can be kept to but are **not always necessary**.
- **Women** may **sit with men in synagogue**.
- **Women** and **men** can become **rabbis**.
- **Women** may wear **tefillin** and **tallit**.

## 5.6 Family life

### Mezuzah

- The **mezuzah** is a **portion** of the **Shema** written on **parchment** and usually placed in a decorative box to keep it clean.
- The Shema is the '**hearing prayer**' found in the Torah which reminds Jews that there is only one God.
- The mezuzah box should be placed on the **right-hand** side of **every door** in the home (except the bathrooms).

- It **shows** that the house is a **Jewish home**.

- It is a reminder to **obey the commandments**.

## Family

Father must:

- **support** his family;

- study **Torah;**

- make sure his **children** study Torah.

Mother must:

- **feed** the family;

- make sure husband and children wear the **right clothes**;

- **prepare** the house for the **Sabbath**;

- **teach daughters** what they need to know about for their homes.

## Food laws

- The **Torah** lays down certain food laws:

- Kosher food means it is 'fit' or **lawful** to be eaten.

- All **blood** must be **removed from meat** before eating it.

- **Meat and milk** products must be **kept separately**.

- **Meat and milk** products must be **eaten separately** (i.e. not in the same meal).

# 5.7 Shabbat

The Shabbat lasts from Friday evening until Saturday evening. It is a day of rest and symbolises God's rest on the seventh day of Creation.

- The **mother** and **children clean and prepare** the house.

- The **Friday evening meal** and other meals are prepared.

- The **mother** lights the **Shabbat candles** and says a special **blessing** just before sunset.

- **Father** (and boys) return **from synagogue**.

- Father says **kiddush** over **wine**.

- The **father** says a **blessing** over two **Hallot loaves** which are then **distributed**.

- The Shabbat **meal is eaten**.

- The **meal ends** with the singing of traditional **Jewish table songs**.

- On **Saturday** the family attend the **synagogue**.

- **Children** may attend **religion school**.

- **No work** is to be done on the Shabbat.

- The **Shabbat ends** with the ceremony of lighting a **special candle**, **smelling spices** and drinking a glass of **wine**.

# 5.8 Birth and Bar Mitzvah

## Birth

The ceremony of circumcision represents a **covenant**, or solemn promise, between God and the child. This remembers the promise made by God to **Abraham**.

- **Boys** must be **circumcised** on the eighth day after birth.

- The ceremony is called **berit milah** and usually takes place at **home**.

- A **mohel** carries out the operation.

- A mohel is a **pious Jew** who is **skilled** at circumcisions.

- After this the child is given his **Hebrew name** and an ordinary name.

- **Kiddush** is said over a cup of **wine**.

- The baby is given a **drop of wine** as his **first kiddush**.

## Bar and Bat Mitzvah

Bar Mitzvah (for boys) and Bat Mitzvah (for girls) are ceremonies which recognise them as adults under the Jewish law. This means that they are responsible for their own actions and must set an example by following the commandments set out in the Torah.

- For a year before a **boy is 13** and a **girl is 12** preparation is given as to their **Jewish responsibilities**.

- On the day of the Bar Mitzvah a **boy reads publicly from the Torah** for the first time in synagogue.

- **Girls** may read from the Torah only in **Reform synagogues**.

- **Boys** may now wear **tefillin** (prayer boxes).

- **Boys** may now wear the **tallit** (prayer shawl).

- **Relatives** attend the synagogue **service**.

- There is often a **party** afterwards.

# 5.9 From marriage to death

## Marriage

Marriage is an important part of traditional Jewish life. Ideally the couple should both be Jewish.

- The bride and groom marry under a **canopy** or **huppah**.

- They are **led** to the **huppah** by their **families**.

- The **bride circles** the **groom**.

- A special **blessing** is made over a cup of **wine** which the **couple sip**.

- The **groom** gives a **ring** to his **bride** in front of **two witnesses**.

- The **rabbi** reads from the **ketubah** or **marriage contract**.

- The choir or cantor **sing** the **seven blessings**.

- The **groom crushes glass** with his foot as a **symbol** of what is **fragile** in life and therefore what **matters** and those present shout 'mozel tov' (congratulations).

## Funeral

- **Orthodox** Jews are always **buried**.

- Some **Reform** Jews allow **cremation**.

- Burial should take place as **soon as possible** but **not** on the **Shabbat**.

- The body is specially **prepared** and **dressed** in a **simple white garment**.

- **After** the **burial** everyone symbolically **washes** their **hands**.

- The bereaved **family** stay at **home** for a **week**.

- **Friends visit**, comfort and bring the mourners food.

- **Men** do not **shave**.

- **Women** do not **wear make-up**.

- At the **first anniversary** of the death a **candle** is lit.

- The special **kaddish** prayer is said in the **synagogue** by the bereaved family.

## 5.10 Rabbis

A **rabbi** is a religious teacher, trained in Jewish law. Reform Jews have women rabbis. Role and duties of a rabbi include:

- Visiting the **sick** and comforting the **bereaved**.

- Taking **marriages** and **funerals**.

- Representing the **community** to the wider community and media.

- Preparing and giving **sermons** in synagogues.

- Giving advice on **conduct**.

- Giving judgements on **Torah** (Law).

- **Leading worship** in the synagogue.

- **Preparing** boys and girls for **Bar/Bat Mitzvah**.

## 5.11 Festivals

Jewish festivals follow the seasons and also remember the history of Israel. They play an important part of the Jewish year. There are many festivals. The following are the most important and popular:

### Pesach/Passover

- **Pesach** is a **spring festival**.

- It remembers the time when **Moses** and the **Israelites** had to **escape** at night from **Egypt**.

- In **preparation** the house is cleaned of all **yeast** or **hametz** products.

- A special **seder** meal is **eaten** before the main meal.

- The **seder begins** when the **youngest child** asks **why this night is different** from all others.

- The story of **Exodus** is **recited** from the **haggadah** or Passover storybook.

- At various parts of the story **four cups** of **wine** are drunk to remember **God's promises**.

- Everyone eats **unleavened bread** or **matzos**.

- Everyone **dips their matzos** into herbs such as **horseradish** and **haroset**.

- Everyone eats an **egg in salt water**.

- Then the **main meal is eaten**.

- **Afterwards** everyone joins in traditional **table songs**.

## Shavuot

- **Shavuot** is a **summer festival**.
- Takes place **50 days after Pesach**.
- It has **many purposes**.
- It remembers when **Moses** received the **Torah at Mount Sinai**.
- It is also a **harvest festival**.
- **Synagogues** and **homes** are **decorated** with **flowers**.
- It is a time to **reflect** on the **gift** of **freedom**.
- It is a time to give **thanks** for the **Torah** and to think about carrying out its **laws**.

## Sukkot

- **Sukkot** is an **autumn festival**.
- Sukkot **remembers** the time when the Israelites **wandered in the Sinai desert**.
- The Israelites built **sukkot** or **tents** to live in.
- Today people **build sukkot** and they can **live** in them for **8 days**.
- The **sukkot** are a reminder of our **dependence** on **God**.
- It is a time to **visit other** people's **sukkot**.
- Sukkot is also a **harvest festival**.
- In the **synagogue** people wave a bundle of **palm**, **myrtle** and **willow** branches and **carry** a **citron fruit**.

## Simchat Torah

- **Simchat Torah** follows the festival of **Sukkot**.
- It means to **rejoice in the Law**.
- It is a time to rejoice that the weekly reading of the Torah is **complete**.
- The **Torah scroll** is **danced** round the inside of the synagogue **seven times**.

## Hanukkah

- Hanukkah is a **winter festival**.
- It is a festival of **light**.
- It remembers the time when the Jews won their **freedom** from the **Greeks** in **164 BCE**.

- It remembers when **Judas Maccabee cleansed the Temple**.

- It remembers how when he lit the **menorah** with enough **oil for one day**, it burnt for **8 days**.

- Today the **Hanukkah lamp** is lit each **evening** for **8 days**.

- It is a time to **exchange presents**.

## Rosh Hashanah

- Rosh Hashanah celebrates the **New Year**.

- It is the beginning of a **10-day period**.

- During this time people **apologise** and seek **forgiveness** from each other.

- It also **remembers** the **creation of the world**.

- People wear their **best clothes**.

- The festival **begins** and **ends** when a ram's horn or **shofar** is **blown**.

- The **last day** is **Yom Kippur**, the **Day of Atonement**.

- Yom Kippur is a time to **fast**, to **attend synagogue** and to **repent** of one's **sins**.

- The **Kol Nidrei** prayer is **sung** at the evening service in the synagogue.

## Purim

- Purim is held in **February/March**.

- It remembers how **Queen Esther saved** the Jewish people from the **evil Haman**.

- Haman drew **lots** (or **purim**) to decide the **day** when all the **Jews** should be **killed**.

- **Esther** bravely **broke the law** and **told** her **husband** of Haman's plan.

- The main part of the synagogue **service** is **reading** the **Esther story**.

- Children **dress up** in masks and costumes to mock Haman.

- Every time **Haman's name** is mentioned people **boo and shout** to **blot out his name**. The children are allowed to bring in pan lids and rattles to do the same.

# Summary

You should now know the following:

1.  The origins and history of Judaism.

2.  The different Jewish holy books.

3.  The central Jewish beliefs.

4.  The role of the synagogue in the Jewish community.

5.  The differences between Orthodox Jews and Reform Jews.

6.  The key beliefs and practices of Jewish family life.

7.  The key beliefs and practices in observing Shabbat.

8.  The key beliefs and practices of birth and bar mitzvah.

9.  The key beliefs and practices of marriage and death.

10. The role of the rabbi.

11. The various Jewish festivals.

# Test yourself

Before moving on to the next chapter, make sure you can answer the following questions. The answers are on pages 183-184.

1.  Describe what happens at a Jewish funeral.     (5)

2.  Describe how Shabbat is celebrated at home.     (5)

3.  Describe what Jews believe about the Torah and the Talmud.     (5)

4.  Describe what Jews believe about the World to Come.     (5)

5.  Describe any **one** important Jewish festival.     (5)

# Chapter 6: World religions: Islam

You only need to revise a minimum of one world religion for the examination. If you are not sure which one to revise, then check with your teacher.

BCE means **Before the Common Era** and is equivalent to using BC.

CE means the **Common Era** and is equivalent to using AD.

In traditional Islam dates are given from the time of the migration to Makkah.

These revision notes follow the order of JF Aylett and Kevin O'Donnell's *The Muslim Experience*. You must make sure that you understand and learn the ideas in *The Muslim Experience* as well as the notes below.

Use ideas from *Study Skills* by Elizabeth Holtom, published by Galore Park, to help you remember these notes and ideas.

## 6.1 God

Muslims (followers of Islam) believe the following about God:

- God's **existence cannot be proved**.
- **God** is the **creator** of everything.
- There are **no other gods**.
- **Only God** may be **worshipped and praised**.
- **God** has **99 beautiful names**.
- All the names are **found** in the **Qur'an**.
- The names describe some of God's **many characteristics**.
- Names include: The **Merciful**, The **Creator**, The **All-Knowing**.
- One of the important **metaphors for God** is **light**.
- **God** will **judge** all people according to their deeds on **earth**.
- **Prayer beads** are a **reminder** of the **99 names**.

## 6.2 Muhammad

Muhammad is regarded by Muslims as the last prophet of God. Muhammad's life and teaching is very important for Muslims as an example of how to live the perfect Muslim life.

## Muhammad's early life

- **Muhammad** was born in **570 CE** in **Makkah**.
- His **father died before** he was **born**, his **mother died** when he was aged **6**.
- Eventually he was **brought up** by an uncle, **Abu Talib**.
- **First** he worked as a **shepherd**.
- He was very **honest** and his **uncle** let him go on **business journeys**.
- He **impressed Khadijah** and she let him **run her business**.
- He **married her** when he was **25**.
- He looked after his **uncle's son Ali**.

## Muhammad's call

- **Muhammad** often went to **pray** in a **cave outside Makkah**.
- He prayed in the cave called **Hira**.
- In **610 CE** when he was **40** the **angel Gabriel** appeared.
- Gabriel told to him to **read** and recite.
- Muhammad **refused three times**.
- The angel squeezed **him three times**.
- Then he **recited God's words**.
- He spent some time in **shock**.
- But he was **reassured by his wife** that he had indeed **received God's word**.

## Muhammad's message

- **Khadijah** and her **cousin** become the **first Muslims**.
- To begin with the **message spread slowly**.
- He **taught** the people of **Makkah not** to **worship idols**.
- This made the **merchants** of **Makkah angry**.
- The merchants considered he was **putting off pilgrims** who also **brought their business** to Makkah.
- They accused Muhammad of being **mad** and a **liar**.
- Some of his **companions** were **tortured** and **killed**.
- In **610 CE** in the vision of the **Night Journey** he met the great **prophets** of the **past**.
- This gave him **confidence** to go on **preaching**.

- Then the people of **Yathrib** asked Muhammad to **come and settle their disputes**.

- In **622 CE** Muhammad, his family and followers went to **Yathrib**.

- The event is called the **hijrah**.

- Here Muhammad started his **first Muslim community**.

- He built his first **mosque**.

- His new laws taught that under **God's rule all people** were to be treated as **equals**.

- **Yathrib** was **renamed Madinah**, or **City of the Prophet**.

## 6.3  The spread of Islam

- Many people were **impressed** by life at **Madinah** and **converted** to Islam.

- Muhammad **marched** on **Makkah** in **630 CE**.

- The Makkans **gave up without** a **fight**.

- Muhammad **removed** all the **idols** from the **Ka'bah**.

- He sent out **letters** to **rulers** to become **Muslim**.

- After **Muhammad's death** in **632 CE Abu Bakr** was appointed **successor** or **caliph**.

- Abu Bakr **united** the tribes of **Arabia**.

- Many **joined** the **Muslims against Byzantine** and **Persian** empires.

- The Muslim empire **spread** to **Africa**, **India** and even reached **China**.

- **Trade spread** Islam further.

Islam is the **principal religion** in the world today in:

- **Northern Africa** – e.g. Morocco, Algeria, Libya and Egypt.

- The **Middle East** – e.g. Iran, Iraq, Saudi Arabia.

- **Indonesia** and **Malaysia**.

# 6.4 Qur'an and Hadith

## The Qur'an

The Qur'an is the central holy book of Islam. Muslims consider it to be the complete revelation of God given to Muhammad by the angel Gabriel. It therefore has very great authority for Muslim beliefs and their way of life.

- **Qur'an** means **recitation**.
- The Qur'an was **revealed** to **Muhammad** by God **through** his angel **Gabriel**.
- It was revealed gradually **over 23 years**.
- It is the **Word of God**.
- **Various people** wrote parts down.
- **Abu Bakr** ordered that a **standard copy** should be made.
- It was **checked** by those who had **heard** it **directly** from **Muhammad**.
- The copy was made less than 2 years after Muhammad died.
- Many **learn** the Qur'an by **heart**.
- These people are called **hafiz**.
- The Qur'an should be **read in Arabic**. If it is translated it ceases to be the **true** and **perfect Word of God**.
- It is God's **final revelation** to humans.

## Qur'an used in worship

- It is given **great respect**.
- When not in use it is kept **wrapped up**.
- It is placed on a **high shelf** to keep it **safe and clean**.
- Everyone must **wash** before reading it.
- It should be **read every day**.
- It should be **obeyed**.

## The Hadith

- The **Hadith** refer to various collections of **books** of the **words and actions** of **Muhammad** himself.
- The Hadith may be consulted by Muslims to see how **Muhammad acted in situations**.

## 6.5 Beliefs

### Five Pillars of Faith

The Five Pillars of Faith refer to the five duties that apply to every Muslim (you do not need to know the Arabic terms).

- **Shahadah**, is the belief in **one God** and that **Muhammad is His messenger**.

- **Alms giving** (zakah) is a form of **tax** to **help** the poor, free people from debt, etc.

- **Prayer** (salah) **five times** a **day** and at the mosque.

- **Fasting** (sawm) performed during **daylight hours** in the month of **Ramadan**.

- **Pilgrimage** (hajj) to **Makkah**.

### Angels

Muslims believe angels to be creatures, made out of light, that exist to only serve God.

- **Angels** are God's **messengers**.

- They bring **God's message** to **humans** especially when they pray.

- They **cannot** usually **be seen**.

- They are made of **light** but can take on **human form**.

- They look after humans and are **felt** as **love and peace**.

### God's books and prophets

Prophets are people appointed by God to guide humans and encourage their faith. Muslims respect the prophets as holy men as examples of the way to live the Muslim life. The most important ones are mentioned by name in the Qur'an.

- God has sent **guidance** through his **prophets**.

- Many have brought special **books** to the world.

- Great prophets include **Adam**, **Noah** and **Abraham**.

- **Moses** brought the **Law**.

- **David** brought the **Psalms**.

- **Jesus** brought the **Gospel**.

- **Muhammad** is the **last prophet**. His message **seals** the **earlier messages**.

- His message is contained in the **Qur'an**.

- Only the **Qur'an** is a **perfect presentation** of God's word.

## Last Judgement and life after death

- Day of Judgement is when all the **dead** will be **judged**.

- Guardian **angels** keep a **record** of every person's deeds.

- Only **God** can **judge** each person's heart.

- The **good** will be rewarded with **Paradise** to a life of **peace** and **purity**.

- **Unbelievers** or the **disobedient** will be sent to **Hell** to a life of **torment**.

- Only **God** knows what is in **Paradise** and what **Hell** is really like.

## The will of God

Muslims believe in the absolute will of God; that is, that God controls all things in the universe.

- God **created** the **world**.

- Everything is **controlled** by God at all times.

- God has **complete knowledge** of everything that happens.

- There is **no** such thing as **chance** as **God controls** the **destiny** of everything.

# 6.6 Salah

Prayer or salah is the fourth pillar of the Five Pillars or duties of Islam.

## When prayer takes place

- Prayers are made **facing** towards the **Ka'bah**.

- **Special prayers** are held on **Friday**.

- **Men** are encouraged to pray in a **mosque**.

- **Women** pray at **home**.

- Prayer can take place in **any clean place**.

- Prayer must come **from the heart**.

- **Praying together** is a sign of Muslim **unity** and **brotherhood**.

- Prayer is a **reminder** of **God's greatness** and **obedience** to Him.

## Preparation

- **Before** prayer a Muslim must perform **wudu**.

- **Wudu** means **washing**.

- The hands, mouth, nose, face, arms, neck, behind ears and feet are washed.

## Daily prayer

Prayer five times a day is compulsory (you do not need to know the Arabic terms).

- Between **dawn and sunrise** (Fajr).

- After **midday** (Zuhr).

- Between late **afternoon and sunset** (Asr).

- Between **sunset and the end of daylight** (Maghrib).

- **Night** (Isha).

- Prayer starts with a series of **prayer movements** called **rakat**.

# 6.7 Mosque

A mosque can be any clean building, which can be used for worship, study and community activities. It should contain a water supply so that each person can wash themselves in preparation for worship or study.

## Role of the muezzin

The **muezzin** is a person, appointed by the mosque, who is responsible for calling out the **adhan** which calls all Muslims to prayer.

- The **muezzin calls** people to **prayer**.

- The **call to prayer** is called the **adhan**.

- The adhan states that '**Allah is the Greatest**; there is no God but Allah'.

- The adhan instructs the people to **rush to prayer**.

- The call is usually done **from** a mosque **minaret**.

- The muezzin faces towards the **Ka'bah** in Makkah.

## Layout of a typical mosque

- There is at **tower** or **minaret** for the **muezzin**.

- There are **wash rooms** and/or fountain for special **washing** or **wudu**.

- In the **prayer hall** there is a **niche** or **mihrab** which indicates the **direction of the Ka'bah**.

- There is often a **dome** over the prayer hall.

- The **pulpit** or **minbar** in a prayer hall is for the **imam** to **preach** and **lead worship**.

- Mosques have **cloakrooms** for **shoes**.

- There are **separate areas** for **men** and **women**.

- There must be **no pictures**.

- The usual decoration are **abstract patterns** and elaborate **extracts** from the **Qur'an**.

## 6.8 Imam

The **imam** is the leader of a Muslim community. He is expected to be a good role model to Muslims.

- The word **imam** means the one who is '**at the front**'.

- He must be of **good moral** standing.

- He must have an excellent **knowledge of Islam**.

- He **leads prayers**.

- He **gives sermons**.

- He looks after the **bereaved**, **gives advice**, **helps in disputes,** etc.

- He may teach **Arabic** in the **mosque school**.

## 6.9 Zakah

The payment of **zakah** is a system whereby wealth is redistributed to the needy. Those who receive the money are most often poor people but can also include newly converted Muslims, or Islamic schools, hospitals and mosques.

- **Zakah** is the **2nd Pillar of Faith**.

- It is a **reminder** that as everything **belongs to God**, material things are on **loan to humans**.

- It is an act of **worship** and a **duty**.

- It is a **test** to ensure that one is **not selfish**.

- Zakah is to be **paid once a year** on 2.5% of one's savings.

- It is usual to give it in **secret** so one **does not get false praise**.

## 6.10 Sawm

**Sawm** or fasting is an act of self-sacrifice, which demonstrates a Muslim's dedication to God.

- **Sawm** is the **4th Pillar of Faith**.

- It occurs during the month of **Ramadan**.

- Fasting is an **act of worship** and **spiritual** development.

- As it involves **suffering** it is a sign of **obedience** to God.

- Fasting helps Muslims to **appreciate the plight of the poor**.

- No food must be eaten from just **before dawn** until just **after sunset**.

- There must be no chewing of food, drinking, smoking or making love.

- Children under 12 **do not** have to **take part**.

- **Actions** as well as the fasting also matter.

- Ramadan gives a feeling of **unity** or **umma** and **common purpose** with other **Muslims**.

# 6.11 Hajj

**Hajj** is a particularly important event in a Muslim's life. Muslims are expected to travel to Makkah and to carry out special rituals there to remind them of their faith.

- **Hajj** is the **5th Pillar of Faith**.

- Every **adult Muslim** is expected to go on **hajj** or **pilgrimage once in a lifetime**.

- When the pilgrims arrive at **Makkah men** change into simple **white clothes**.

- This is a state of **spiritual purity** or **ihram**.

- On the **1st day** pilgrims **circle** the **Ka'bah seven times**.

- Pilgrims then **run between** the **two hills** and the **Zamzam** well.

- Next they **camp out** overnight at **Muzdalifah**.

- The next day pilgrims stand in the **Plain of Arafat** and spend the day in **prayer** and **meditation**.

- On the following day they **throw stones** at the **pillars of Mina** to drive out Satan.

- On returning to **Muzdalifah** they **sacrifice** an **animal**.

- **Men** often **shave their heads**.

- Then they return to **Makkah** and **circle Ka'bah** one last time.

- Someone who has been on pilgrimage is called a **hajji**.

# 6.12 Birth and death

## Birth

- At the **birth** the **father whispers** the call to prayer or **adhan** into the baby's **right ear**.

- Softened **date or honey** is **rubbed** onto the baby's **gums**.

- **Seven days** later the baby's **head is shaved**, This is called **aqiqah**.

- The baby is given a **name**.

- Names often combine **Abd**, meaning servant, with **one of God's 99 names**.

- **Boys** are then **circumcised**.

- It is a time of **celebration**.

## Death

- Muslims believe in **life after death**.

- The dead person's **body** is **washed**, **anointed** and wrapped in **white sheets**.

- **Burial** takes place **as soon as possible**.

- The person is **buried** (cremation is forbidden) with their **head facing the Ka'bah**.

- As the body is **buried** the **Qur'an is recited** and earth thrown in the grave.

- A period of **mourning** follows.

# 6.13 Marriage

Islam regards marriage as a duty. Some couples marry when they consider themselves to be ready but for others, parents might help to find a suitable partner.

- Marriages are **often arranged**. Love is not a primary reason for marriage.

- **Parents find** a suitable **bride/groom** for their son/daughter.

- The **husband** gives his **wife** a **dowry**, i.e. a sum of money.

- At the **wedding** people wear their **best clothes**.

- The wedding can take place at the **mosque or bride's house**.

- **Two witnesses** have to be present at the signing of the **wedding contract**.

- Passages from the **Qur'an** are **recited**.

- A **feast** is given for the relatives within three days **following the marriage**.

- **Divorce** is allowed but only as a **last resort**.

- **Men** may marry up to **four wives** but this is **rare**.

## 6.14 Family life

### Roles of men and women in the family

- **Both** parents must set an **example** to their **children**.

- Parents must **educate** and **feed** their **children** properly.

- **Both** parents must **respect their own parents** and be **obedient** to them.

- **Mothers** have a **responsibility** to **feed** the hungry, **look after** guests, **comfort** the distressed.

- **Husbands** must **provide money, protect** the family and be involved in the **wider world**.

- **Both** must **dress modestly**.

- There must be **no sex before marriage**.

### Children's attitude to parents

- Children must **respect parents**.

- Children must be **obedient** to their **parents** and **older relatives**.

- **No child** should **cause harm** to his or her parents.

- In old age **parents** may need to be **supported by children**.

- This duty **continues** until **parents' deaths**.

## 6.15 Festivals

### Id-ul-Fitr

- The festival was **started** by **Muhammad**.

- It marks the **end of Ramadan**.

- It is also a time to **thank God** for the **Qur'an**.

- Muslims thank God for **getting through Ramadan**.

- Many give a special Ramadan **zakat** or **money to the poor**.

- **Children** are given **presents**.

- There is **no work or school**.

- A **special midday meal** is eaten.

- It is also a special time to go to the **mosque** to **pray**.

### Id-ul-Adha

- The festival takes place **towards** the **end of the Hajj**.
- It is **also** celebrated by **those not on hajj**.
- **Id-ul-Adha** remembers when **Abraham** was ready to **sacrifice Ishmael**.
- Abraham was willing to sacrifice him because **God commanded** it.
- He **resisted the temptations** of the **devil** not to sacrifice Ishmael.
- This shows that **Muslims** must be **ready** to **sacrifice their lives** for God.
- The festival **begins** with **prayers** at the **mosque**.
- An **animal** is **sacrificed** to remember Abraham's sacrifice of an animal.
- The **meat** is **shared** with friends, relatives and the poor.

## Summary

You should now know the following:

1. What Muslims believe about God.
2. The role of Muhammad.
3. How Islam spread.
4. The content of the Qur'an and Hadith.
5. The central Islamic beliefs.
6. The way Muslims pray.
7. The role of the mosque in the Muslim community.
8. The role of imam.
9. The importance of zakah.
10. The importance of sawm.
11. What happens when a Muslim goes on hajj.
12. The Muslim teaching on birth and death.
13. The Muslim teaching on marriage.
14. The Muslim teaching on Muslim family life.
15. The main Muslim festivals.

## Test yourself

Before moving on to the next chapter, make sure you can answer the following questions. The answers are on page 184.

1. Describe what happened at Muhammad's call. (5)

2. Describe what Muslims believe about the Qur'an and Hadith. (5)

3. Explain what Muslims believe about angels. (5)

4. Describe what happens on Hajj (pilgrimage). (5)

5. Describe the roles of men and women in the Muslim family. (5)

# Chapter 7: World religions: Hinduism

You only need to revise a minimum of one world religion for the examination. If you are not sure which one to revise, then check with your teacher.

BCE means **Before the Common Era** and is equivalent to using BC.

CE means the **Common Era** and is equivalent to using AD.

These revision notes follow the order of Liz Aylett and Kevin O'Donnell's *The Hindu Experience*. You must make sure that you understand and learn the ideas in *The Hindu Experience* as well as the notes below.

Use the ideas in *Study Skills* by Elizabeth Holtom, published by Galore Park, to help you remember these notes and ideas.

## 7.1 Origins

You will be expected to know the following about the origins and history of Hinduism.

- **Hindus** believe that their religion has **always existed**.

- This idea is called **Sanatana Dharma** or **Eternal Law**.

- Hinduism has **developed** over thousands of years.

- Hinduism has it **beginnings** in the **Indus valley**.

- **Some** were **polytheists**, who believed in **many deities** or gods.

- **Some** worshipped the deities as **aspects** of the **one God**.

- **Some** were **monotheists** who believed in **one God**.

- **Evidence** of earliest Hindu **advanced civilisation** has been found in the city of **Mohenjo-daro**.

- The **city** had complex **drainage** systems and pipes for **running water**.

- Many appeared to worship the **mother goddess**.

- They **buried** their **dead** and made offerings to gods and goddesses.

- About **3500 years** ago **Aryans** came from the **north**.

- The **Aryans** used **fire** as the chief symbol of **worship**.

- Their worship of the **sky gods** developed a more **abstract** form of **religion**.

- One of their **main gods** was **Indra**, the god of **Thunder**.

- The **Aryans married** the local people and their **religion mixed** with the **ancient religion** of the Indus valley.

## 7.2 Growth

- The next stage of **development** was through the **holy men**.

- The holy men or monks practised **meditation**.

- The holy men lived in **forests** and **supported each other**.

- **Disciples visited** the holy men and were **taught** by them.

- The holy men developed the **idea** of **Brahman**.

- **Brahman** is the idea that there is **one unifying force** of nature and the universe.

- **Sometimes Brahman** is thought to be **personal**, **sometimes** it is abstract and **impersonal**.

- In **meditation** the word **aum** is used to refer to **Brahman**.

- The worship of a **personal God** is called **bhakti**.

- The path or **way to God** is called **yoga**.

- The holy men developed **several forms** of **meditation** to **develop yoga**.

## 7.3 Holy books

The holy books of Hinduism are written in Sanskrit, an ancient language. The holy books fall into two kinds: the **Vedas** (the oldest) and the **Smirtis** (the commentaries and reflections on the Vedas) The **Bhagavad Gita** is one chapter of the Mahabharata (a very long and popular Hindu story).

### Vedas

- The **Vedas** are the **oldest** of the Hindu **holy books**.

- **Veda** means **knowledge** because they **come from God**.

- They provide **knowledge** of the **world**.

- They contain **hymns** and **prayers** for **priests** to sing.

- Originally they were **learnt by heart** but later they were **written down**.

- There are **four collections** of Vedas.

- The **Rig Veda** is the most **important**.

## Upanishads

The **Upanishads** are part of the **Vedas**, but are often considered important enough to be classed on their own.

- The **Upanishads** are written as **questions and answers** from **pupils to teachers**.

- They are **poems** written by the **holy men**.

- They **meditate** on God as **Brahman**.

- They meditate on the **meaning life** and **reincarnation**.

## Smirtis

- The **holy men** wrote **commentaries** on the **Vedas** to explain them.

- These are called **smirtis**.

- They were written **2500 years** ago.

- They are **not** always **easy** to **understand**.

- Simpler books were written containing stories.

- The **Ramayana** is a collection of **stories** and **poems** about the **ancient heroes**.

- Another **important story** is the **Mahabharata**.

## The Mahabharata

The **Mahabharata** is **smirti**. It is one of the longest poems ever produced.

- The story tells the **history** of ancient **India**.

- Eldest **Kuru** brother, Dhritavashtra, was **blind** so could **not rule effectively**.

- Instead his **brother Pandu became king**.

- But Pandu wanted to be a **holy man**.

- So he **gave** the **kingdom** back to his **brother**.

- Dhritavashtra looked after **Pandu's five sons**.

- But his **own sons** became very **jealous** and wanted to **kill Pandu's sons**.

- Pandu's sons escaped to the **forest led by Prince Arjuna**.

- The **blind king gave Pandu's sons half his kingdom** but the **Kurus stole it**.

- A **great battle** followed between the **Kurus** and **Pandavas** (the **sons of Pandu**).

- The **Pandavas won** and **ruled wisely**.

- The story is about the **battle** between **good and evil**.

## Bhagavad Gita

The **Bhagavad Gita** is a very influential Hindu scripture. It forms part of the **Mahabharata** (it is therefore smirti) and is the most philosophical part of it.

- The **Bhagavad Gita** forms one **chapter** of the **Mahabharata**.

- It means **Song of the Lord**.

- It is a **poem** in which **Arjuna** is about to **enter** the **battle** but does not want to kill his own relations.

- **Arjuna** turns to **Krishna** for **advice**.

- **Krishna** is in the form of his **chariot driver** and **teaches** him.

- **Krishna** then **reveals himself as God**.

- He tells **Arjuna** that he must **fulfil** his **duty** as a prince and **fight**.

- He explains that **no one can kill** the **soul**.

- He explains that **life** is only **worthwhile** in **loving and worshipping God**.

- **Arjuna** goes on to **fight** and **win**.

# 7.4  Beliefs

## Brahman

Hindu philosophers believe that God or **Brahman** is the ultimate Reality of the universe. It can be experienced in many different ways and takes on the form of many deities which are worshipped separately by Hindus.

- Hindus believe in **one God** who manifests himself in **many forms**.

- The **forms** are the **deities** such as **Vishnu**, **Shiva**, **Durga** or **Krishna**.

- **Brahman** is the **invisible** aspect of God.

- **Aum** represents the **mystical vibration** of God/Spirit in the universe.

- **Brahman** is this **spirit or life-force**.

- **Brahman** is the **origin of everything**.

- **Brahman** is in **everything** but **cannot be seen**.

- **Brahman** is both **personal** or **impersonal**.

- The **worship of Brahman** is called **bhakti**.

## Atman and Samsara

- **Every** living **thing** has **atman**.

- **Atman** is **soul** and is **part of Brahman**.

- That means we **all** have an **aspect of God within** us.

- When the body of a living thing **dies,** its **atman moves on** to **another body**.

- This is called **samsara** or **reincarnation**.

- **Samsara** also describes the **changes we go through in life** as our bodies change.

- Our **characters** may change but deep down we are the **same person** or **atman**.

## Karma

- **Karma** is the **law of cause and effect**.

- Karma affects **samsara** and how we behave in a **reincarnated life**.

- A **good life** now means the **next life** will be **happier or better**.

- A **bad life** now means the **next life** will be **unhappier or unlucky**.

- **Bad karma** could even result in being reincarnated as a **lower life form**.

## Dharma

- **Dharma** means **duty** and to do what is **morally right**.

- **Dharma** is informed by **conscience** and the **scriptures**.

- **Dharma** also describes Hinduism as **Eternal Truth**.

## Ahisma

- **Ahisma** means **non-violence**.

- As all living things have **atman** so all must be **treated with respect**.

- Sometimes this causes **moral problems**.

- **Arjuna** had to decide between his **duty not to harm** and **his duty to fight against evil**.

## Environment

- Hindus believe we should all be **grateful** for **God's gifts in nature**.

- All **living things** have a soul or **atman**.

- So **humans** have a responsibility to **look after nature**.

- Humans must only accept those things **given to them**.

- **Earth** is 'our mother' and **humans** 'her children'.

- **Offerings** should be given to **sacred areas in nature**.

- **Killing living things** can result in **bad karma**.

## Cows and vegetarianism

- **Cows** are **sacred** because they provide for **human needs**.

- They provide **milk**.

- They provide **butter**.

- The provide **ghee** used for **offerings to the deities**.

- They pull **carts**.

- They are seen as '**mothers**'.

- They are a **gift from God**.

- **Respect** for the **cow** and other **living beings** means Hindus should be **vegetarians**.

# 7.5 Caste and dharma

Hindu society is divided into **four** social groupings called **castes** or **varnas**. Each caste has specific duties that a person is expected to carry out if they are to gain good **karma**.

- Each caste is associated with **specific jobs** or roles.

- **Brahmins** are **priests** and **teachers**.

- **Kshatriyas** are **rulers** and **fighters**.

- **Vaishyas** are **farmers** and **traders**.

- **Shudras** are **workers**.

- **Untouchables** are 'casteless' and not members of the varnas.

- Each caste has specific **duties** or **dharma** it has to carry out.

- Carrying out one's caste duties affects one's **karma** and therefore one's **caste in the next life**.

- It is **illegal in India today** to **discriminate** against someone because of their **caste**.

- Some teach a **more spiritual version** of the varnas which says you can **change caste** by developing different **attitudes** and **skills**.

## 7.6 Goal

Hindus believe that every living thing has a goal to reach during a lifetime, and it is the duty of everyone to try to obtain it by following Hindu teaching.

- **Moksha** is the **goal of life**.

- **Moksha** means **release** from **samsara** – the **cycle of rebirths**.

- When the soul or **atman** is **pure** it is **released** to become **one with God**.

- There are **three paths** to moksha:

  - The way of **action**, good works or **karma**;

  - The way of **knowledge** or **jnana**;

  - The way of **devotion** or **bhakti**.

- **Moksha** is also achieved through **meditation** and **bodily control** or **raja**.

## 7.7 God

Hindus believe in only **one God**. However, this God has many different **aspects** that cause him to take on different **forms**.

- Although there is **one God** he can appear and be worshipped in **many forms**.

- **Some** believe all gods are **forms** of **Brahman**.

- Each god/form represents **an aspect of God**.

- Each Hindu is a **devotee** to a **particular form**.

- The most **popular** deities are **Vishnu** and **Shiva**.

### Gods/forms and their symbols

### Brahma

- **Brahma** is **symbolised** by **fire** and the sound **aum**.

### Vishnu

- Some worship **Vishnu** as the supreme form of God.

- He is **preserver** of the cosmos.

- He is an aspect of **Supreme Being** or **Brahman**.

- His **four arms** symbolise **power**.

- His **conch** shell symbolises **worship**.

- He comes to earth in **10** various **forms** or **avatars**.

- **Six avatars** are **animal** or semi-human, **four are human**.

- Avatars include the **dwarf**, **Rama** and **Krishna**.
- **Lesser deities** are called **mahatmas** or **great souls**.

## Shiva

- Some worship **Shiva** as the supreme form of God.
- He is shown as a **dancing figure**.
- His **dance** symbolises the **power of creation**.
- He holds a **drum** which symbolises the **rhythm of life**.
- The **ring of fire** which surrounds him symbolises his **power to create and destroy**.

## Paths to God

The **Paths to God** represent the three ways in which a person can achieve **moksha**, or their release from the cycle of samsara (reincarnation).

- The **three paths** are: **karma**, **jnana** and **bhakti**.
- That means as God is **active** we must offer our hard **work** to God.
- That means as God is **knowledge** we must offer our **minds** to God.
- That means as God is **love** we must offer our **worship** to God.

# 7.8 From birth to death

Hindus divide a lifetime up into stages, which correspond with an important event in a person's life. Some stages are marked with a religious ceremony.

- Each **stage of life** is called a **samskara**.
- There are **16 samskaras**.

## Birth

- When a **baby is born** the **priest** works out a **horoscope** to see how the planets will affect the person's life.
- The horoscope tells the parents which **letter** their **child's name** should begin with.
- Some **choose names** after the **gods or deities** such as Lakshmi or Krishna.

## Initiation or the sacred thread ceremony

- This takes place for a **boy** sometime between his **8th and 11th birthday**.
- This is the **10th samskara**.
- The ceremony is only for those boys who belong to the **first three castes** or varnas.
- The **thread** consists of **three strands** (white, red, yellow) and are reminders of the boy's **three duties**:
  - **1st** duty to **God**;
  - **2nd** duty to his **parents**;
  - **3rd** duty to his religious **teachers**.
- The **ceremony** is held at **home**.
- The **thread** is put over his **left shoulder**.
- It is **placed** there by his **priest or teacher**.
- He will **wear it all his life**.
- It is a **sign** that he is now an **adult**.

## Marriage

- It is a **duty** of Hindu **men to marry**.
- Marriages are often **arranged**.
- **Love develops** later in a relationship.

## Wedding preparations of the bride

- The bride **bathes in perfumed water**.
- She rubs her skin with **turmeric powder**.
- She wears her **best sari**.
- She **paints patterns** on her hands with **henna**.

## Wedding ceremony

- **Weddings** often take place at **night**.
- At the ceremony the couple take **seven steps** around a **fire**, which represents **God's presence**.
- This symbolises their hope for **children**, **wealth**, **happiness**, etc.
- As they do this they **carry a scarf** to symbolise how their lives are **joined together**.
- The **final step** marks the moment when they become **husband and wife**.

- **Rice grain** is sprinkled over the couple as a sign of **fertility**.

- Afterwards some couples put their **handprints on the bride's parents** house as **sign** that she has **left home**.

## Death

- Some men choose **to stay as householders** but when the children have left home they devote more time to God and go on **pilgrimage**.

- Some **give** up **all home life** and become **sanyasi**.

- This is the **14th samskara**.

- When a person **dies** their body is **washed** and dressed in **fresh clothes**.

- **Flowers** are put round the body.

- The **16th samskara** is cremation when the body is put on a **funeral pyre**.

- The **ashes** should be **scattered** in **a holy river**.

- Cremation **releases the soul** for its next stage of its journey.

# 7.9 Pilgrimage

Pilgrimage is the act of making a journey to a place that has a special relevance to a religious belief. People who make them are known as **pilgrims**. Hinduism regards pilgrimage as a way of proving dedication to God or a particular deity.

- Most pilgrimages **end** with a visit to a **temple**.

- There are **many temples** but the important ones are **Badrinath, Rameshwaram, Puri** and **Dwarka**.

- Pilgrimage is a sign of **religious dedication** as it costs time and money.

- Pilgrimage is **social** but **also** a time of **spiritual cleansing**.

- Some visit **special places** like the river **Ganges** and the holy city of **Varanasi**.

- Some visit **Jagannath** where there is a huge **image** of **Krishna**.

# 7.10 Festivals

Hindu festivals celebrate the different seasons of the year, as well as some of the stories of the Indian heroes.

## New Year

- It is usually celebrated in **March/April**.
- Many **families** make a **banner** and hang it above the door.
- Some make **Rangoli** or special **patterns** outside their houses to welcome the New Year.

## Dassehra

- Celebrated towards the end of **October**.
- **Remembers** the story of **Rama**.
- Many **act out** the story.
- Some make **models** of the evil **Ravana**, which they smash.
- Some **burn** large pictures of **Ravana** filled with **fireworks**.

## Divali

- It takes place in late **autumn**.
- It lasts **2–5 days**.
- People light **oil lamps** or **Divas**.
- The **lamps** are placed on **window ledges/doors**.
- The **light** remembers how **Rama** was **welcomed home** after he **defeated Ravana**.
- The **lights** are also to welcome **Lakshmi** to people's homes.
- The Divali is the **story recited** to remember how evil was destroyed by good.
- Many set off **fireworks**.

## Holi

- Holi is a **spring festival**.
- It is named after evil **Princess Holika**.
- She tried to **kill her nephew** but was burned in a fire.
- Large **bonfires** are lit on the **eve** of the festival.
- **Krishna's** life is **remembered**.
- The **morning after** is a time for **practical jokes**.
- **Children** are allowed to be **cheeky to adults**.

# 7.11 Worship at home

Most Hindus perform worship at home once or twice a day.

- **Worship** is called **puja**.
- **Families** are usually **devoted** to **one** particular **deity**.
- Many have a **shrine** at home.
- The **shrine** contains images of the **family's** favourite **deity** or **deities**.
- **Each day** the deity is **woken up** and a **lamp** is **lit**.
- The image or **murti** is **washed** and **dressed**.
- **Flowers** are offered and **incense** burned.
- Special **food** is **offered** and **blessed**.
- **Prashad** (blessed food) is **eaten** by the **family**.
- **Prayers** may be in the form of a **mantra** or chant.
- Some practise **yoga** or **meditation** instead.
- At the **end of the day puja** is performed and the image is **put away** for the **night**.

# 7.12 Temple

The temple is the centre of Hindu worship outside of the home.

## Typical temple

- A temple is **dedicated** to a particular **god/goddess**.
- It is the **home** of the deity's **image** or **murti**.
- The temple is sometimes called a **mandir**.
- A **priest's** role is to **look after** the **murti**.
- Every day he **prepares** the **murti** ready **for worshippers**.
- The **temple** is **built** to symbolise the meeting of **heaven and earth**.
- The temple **spires** also symbolise the **journey of the soul to moksha**.
- It contains **carvings** from the **animal**, **human** and **divine worlds**.
- It is usually very **tall** like a **mountain range**.
- The **porch** contains the 'vehicle' or **vihara** of the deity.
- The **main hall** or **mandapa** often has **pillars**.
- The **inner shrine**, the '**womb**' or **shikara**, contains the **image** of the deity.

### Worship in the temple

- **Worship** in the temple is very similar to **puja at home**.

- People take their **shoes off** before entering the **mandapa**.

- Each person **rings a bell** to **tell** the **deity** that they have **arrived**.

- Some **pray** by **themselves** or in **family groups**.

- Some people **meditate quietly**, others **sing hymns or prayers**.

- **Hindu scriptures** are read at various times.

- The **priest** performs **arti** by passing round a lamp and people place their hands near it.

- The **light** and **fire** symbolise the **presence of the deity**.

- The **priest** makes **daily offerings** of **incense**, **fire** and **water**.

- The **worshippers offer gifts** of **money**, **food** and **flowers**.

- The **priest** offers worshippers **prashad** in return.

- The **priest** prepares the **deity** for the **night**.

## Summary

You should now know the following:

1. The origins and history of Hinduism.

2. The growth of Hinduism.

3. The different holy books

4. The key Hindu beliefs.

5. The importance of castes and dharma.

6. The significance of moksha or goal of life.

7. Belief of God in Hinduism.

8. A person's lifetime, from birth to death.

9. The key events of pilgrimages.

10. The various Hindu festivals.

11. How Hindus worship at home.

12. The role of the temple in Hindu life.

# Test yourself

Before moving on to the next chapter, make sure you can answer the following questions. The answers are on page 185.

1. Describe the story in the Mahabharata. (5)

2. Explain the Hindu teaching on atman and samsara (reincarnation). (5)

3. Describe **one** Hindu festival. (5)

4. Describe what happens at a typical Hindu wedding. (5)

5. Describe worship in a Hindu temple. (5)

# Chapter 8: World religions: Buddhism

You only need to revise a minimum of one world religion for the examination. If you are not sure which one to revise, then check with your teacher.

> **BCE** means **Before the Common Era** and is equivalent to using BC.
>
> **CE** means the **Common Era** and is equivalent to using AD.

These revision notes follow the order of Mel Thompson's *The Buddhist Experience*. You must make sure that you understand and learn the ideas in *The Buddhist Experience* as well as the notes below.

Use the ideas in *Study Skills* by Elizabeth Holtom, published by Galore Park, to help you remember these notes and ideas.

## 8.1 Siddhartha

**Siddhartha**, who became the **Buddha**, is the central figure of **Buddhism**. His example is sometimes used as a parable to show how a person can live their lives and aim for enlightenment.

- **Siddhartha's father** was **ruler** of the **Northern Indian** clan.
- He was **brought up** in **luxury**.
- A **wise man** said **Siddhartha** would grow up to be a **religious teacher**.
- He would give **away all his possessions** and **power**.
- He **trained** in the **martial arts**.
- He **married** at a young age and had a **child**.
- His **father stopped** him seeing what lay **outside** the **palace**.
- He gave him every **luxury** so **Siddhartha wouldn't** be **interested** in **religion**.

### Siddhartha's quest

- **Siddhartha** was not happy and **wanted** to **see outside** the palace.
- He set out from his palace and saw **four sights**:
  - **First** an **old person**;
  - **Second** a **sick person**;
  - **Third** a **dead person**;
  - **Fourth** a **holy man**.

- **Siddhartha** set out as a **homeless wanderer** at the age of **29**.

- He lived a life of **prayer** and **ate almost nothing** as the life of an **ascetic**.

- But **after 6 years** he realised that this did **not bring enlightenment**.

## The Enlightened One

- **Siddhartha** was **abandoned** by his **five companions**.

- He **sat** at the **foot** of a **Bo-Tree**.

- He **vowed** he would **stay there** until he had **discovered** the **truth**.

- He experienced many **temptations** throughout the **night**.

- He saw **visions** of things of the **past**, his many **previous lives** and **suffering**.

- At **dawn** he believed he had achieved **enlightenment**.

- He now realised the **cause of suffering** is caused by **craving**.

- He now realised that **everything affects everything** else.

- He now realised that everything **changes**, including ourselves.

- He was now called the **Buddha** or **Enlightened One**.

# 8.2 Dharma

**Dharma** is the term used for the **Buddha's teaching**. It means the 'Path of Awakening' and, by following it, Buddhists hope to achieve **enlightenment**. Make sure you understand that the Noble Eightfold Path is also the fourth truth of the Four Noble Truths.

## Three Universal Truths

- The **First Truth is anicca**: everything **changes**.

- Everything changes because everything is **dependent** on everything else.

- The **Second Truth is anatta**: there is **no enduring self or soul**.

- We have **no souls** because people change and things change.

- The **Third Truth is dukkha**: there is **suffering** because everything changes, things **die**.

## Four Noble Truths

The Four Noble Truths were among the first things taught by the Buddha soon after his enlightenment.

- **First**: all life involves **suffering** or **dukkha**.

- **Second**: the origin of suffering is **craving** or **tanha**.

- **Third**: if **craving goes** so does suffering.

- **Fourth**: the **Middle Way** or Eightfold Path is the middle way between extremes.

- The **extremes** are **luxury** and **hardship**.

- **Extremes do not bring enlightenment**, only the middle way does.

## The Noble Eightfold Path

As the Fourth Noble Truth, the **Noble Eightfold Path** sets out the way in which a follower may bring **suffering** or **dukkha** to an end.

- The Noble Eightfold Path is the middle path **between extremes**.

- It is the **fourth** element of the **Four Noble Truths**.

- The path gives advice for **everyday living**.

- The path also helps **train the mind** with the:

  - Right **view**;

  - Right **intention**;

  - Right **speech**;

  - Right **action**;

  - Right **livelihood**;

  - Right **effort**;

  - Right **mindfulness**;

  - Right **contemplation**.

## Karma

- **Karma** is the **law** of **cause and effect**.

- Actions have **consequences** on **oneself** and **others**.

- Now and in **future** lives.

- The **Noble Eightfold Path** gives **guidance** to be aware of **karma**.

## The Triple Way

- Way 1: **Morality** – how to treat **others**.

- Way 2: **Meditation** – how to **think** clearly.

- Way 3: **Wisdom** – how to **reflect** on one's life.

### Nirvana

- **Rebirth** occurs when a person lives a **life** of **greed** and **ignorance** ('the fires').

- **Nirvana** is a state when greed and **ignorance** are no longer experienced.

- **Nirvana** means '**blowing out**'.

- **Nirvana** is a state of **contentment**.

- **Nirvana** can only be **achieved** when **enlightened**.

## 8.3 Sangha

**Sangha** refers to the worldwide **community** of Buddhists. The Sangha for monks and nuns have special rules and duties to help each person to achieve enlightenment.

- The **first followers** of **Buddha** were called the **Sangha**.

- All **members** are **equal**.

- **Sangha** gives **support** to all to achieve **enlightenment**.

- **Some** choose to become **monks** or **bhikkhus**.

- **Some** choose to become **nuns** or **bhikkhunis**.

- **Monks study** the **Dharma** in Buddhist **monasteries** or **viharas**.

- **Monks** and **nuns** have a special **responsibility** to **teach Dharma**.

- **Sangha also refers** to the worldwide community of **all Buddhists**.

## 8.4 Types of Buddhism

- Most traditions **distinguish** between Buddhist **monks/nuns** and ordinary or **lay** Buddhists.

- The **Three main traditions** are: **Theravada**, **Mahayana** (Pure Land and Zen) and **Tibetan**.

- **Western** Buddhism is a mixture of all three traditions.

### Theravada Buddhism

Theravada is the oldest form of Buddhism that is still followed today.

- **Theravadan** Buddhism places **importance** on the practice of **meditation**.

- It considers that being a **monk** is an **ideal** way of being a Buddhist.

- **Monks** wear **saffron robes**.

- They **shave** their **heads**.

- They live in **monasteries**.

- They receive **food** from **lay people**.
- They use **beads** for **meditation**.
- Many become **lay monks** for a while to **learn Dharma** and then **leave** the monastery.

## Mahayana Buddhism

Mahayana Buddhism was probably formed in Southern India in the 1st century CE.

- **Mahayanan** Buddhism is aimed at **lay people** not just monks/nuns.
- **Pure Land Buddhism** believes in devotion to **Amida Buddha**.
- They chant '**Nembutsu**' as a form of **meditation**.
- They think this will **help** them **enter 'Buddha Land'** a state free from troubles.
- **Zen Buddhism** is popular in **Japan**.
- **Zen** teaches that **everyone** has a **Buddha nature**.
- It is through **training** the **mind** that a person can **discover** their Buddha nature.
- Zen teaches us to be **aware of every action**.
- **Awareness** can be **achieved** through **simple actions** such as having tea and **arranging flowers**.

## Tibetan Buddhism

Tibetan Buddhism is similar to Mahayanan Buddhism in that it is not just aimed at monks and nuns. However, it takes a different approach to worship.

- **Tibetan** Buddhism stresses the **importance** of **images** and wall-hangings for **meditation**.
- It uses **chants** or **mantras** in worship.
- There is often a lot of use of **dancing**, **music** and **processions** at **festivals**.
- They use **prayer wheels**.
- The **monks** are very keen on **debates** in monasteries.
- **Senior teachers** are called **lamas**.
- The most **famous lama** is the **Dalai Lama**.

### Western Buddhism

Buddhism spread to the West mostly through Indian and Chinese immigrants during the 20th century.

- **All types** of Buddhism are practised in the West.
- **Friends of the Western Buddhist Order** (FWBO) **mixes** all three **traditions**.
- The FWBO **adapts** the three traditions for use in the West.
- People who first join are called '**Friends**'.
- FWBO does **not have monks/nuns**.
- **Some** live in **single sex communities**.
- **Many** continue to live in their **own families**.

## 8.5  Refuge

A solemn **declaration** is made by a person when they become a Buddhist. 'Taking refuge' means making three promises to live according to the principles of Buddhism.

- It means to **face life** and to put the **Buddha's teaching** into **practice**.
- It marks a **moment** when a person **chooses** the **Buddhist way of life**.
- Said in front of an **ordained Buddhist**:
    - '**I go to the Buddha**';
    - '**I go to the Dharma**';
    - '**I go to the Sangha**'.
- **Offerings** are made of **candles, flowers** and **incense**.
- A Buddhist **promises** to live a life of **compassion** for other **humans**.
- A Buddhist **promises** to help and **respect all creatures**.

## 8.6  Buddha images

The Buddha is never worshipped in Buddhism. But the various images are very helpful for **education** and **meditation**.

### Use of images

- **Some** images are of the **historical Buddha**.
- **Some** images are **symbols** of the **inner experiences** of the Buddha.
- Images are used to **help** in **meditation**.

- **Some** images are **expressions** of **bodhisattvas,** that is all those who have become **enlightened**.

- **Some** Buddhists like to **meditate** using **several images**.

- **Some** meditate just using an image of the **historical Buddha**.

## Types of images

- The **angry Buddha** helps to direct **anger** in a **positive way**.

- **Bodhisattva Manjogosha** shows how the **sword of wisdom cuts** through **ignorance**.

- **Yab-Yum** picture of a sexual couple shows a **relationship** of **wisdom** and **compassion**.

## Symbols

- The **flame** from Buddha's head is a symbol of **enlightenment**.

- An image with **1000 arms** symbolises the **help** given by a **bodhisattva** in any situation.

- An image of **stepping down** is a symbol of the way a **bodhisattva** comes to **help** people.

- A **vajra** or **thunderbolt** is a sign of **determination**.

- A **lotus flower** is a sign of **enlightenment**.

- The lotus is a symbol of the journey of the mind from **ignorance** to **wisdom**.

- The **eight-spoked wheel** represents the **eightfold path** that life **comprises change** and **stillness**.

# 8.7 At a shrine or temple

For some Buddhists the temple is the centre of worship outside of the home. The temple contains a shrine room, in which Buddhist imagery is found. A home may also have a shrine to the Buddha.

## Worship or puja

- In the **temple** there is often much chanting of spiritual sayings or **mantras**.

- A common mantra is: **Om mani padme hum**.

- **Offerings** are made to the **image of a Buddha**.

- Devotees **listen** to the Buddhist **scriptures**.

## A shrine might include

- **Buddha images**.
- **Seven offering bowls** set in **front** of the **Buddha image**.
- **Flowers**, **candles** and **incense**, which are traditional **offerings**.
- **Cushions** for **meditation**.
- A **bell** to tell when the **next stage** of **puja** is to start.

## Types of shrines/temple

- **Monuments** or **stupas** contain a **relic** of the **Buddha**, such as a part of his clothing, etc.
- **Pilgrims** walk **round the outside** of monuments.
- **Temples** have **rooms** for **chanting** and **meditating**.
- In a **shrine room people** turn to the shrine and put their **hands together** as a sign of **respect**.
- **Shrines at home** might also have a **Buddha image**, **flowers** and **incense**.

# 8.8 Festivals

There are **no fixed rules** for Buddhist festivals, and the festival **ceremonies** are **not essential**. Festivals are helpful though in developing a pure **state of mind** and sense of fellowship or 'buddhahood'.

## Festival of Wesak

- **Wesak** is celebrated at **full moon** in **May**.
- It remembers the **birth of the Buddha**.
- It celebrates the **Buddha's enlightenment** and **death**.
- There are **joyful processions**.
- People **decorate** their **local shrines** and **homes**.

## Festival of New Year

- It is mostly celebrated in **Thailand** in **April**.
- **Water** is used to wash **Buddha images**.
- People **splash each other**.
- **Stranded fish** are **put back** into **rivers**.
- **Water** is used because it is a **symbol** of **new life** and **refreshment**.

### Festival of the Full Moon

- Celebrates the **beginning** of the **Buddha's teaching** or **dharma**.

### Festival of Kathina

- **Monks** and **nuns** go on **retreat**.
- People make **offerings** of **practical things** to the **monasteries**.

# 8.9 Buddhist way of life

## The Five Precepts or skills

The Five Precepts govern how a Buddhist ought to live if he or she is to achieve a balanced life and perhaps even enlightenment.

- Avoid **taking life**.
- Avoid **taking what is not given**.
- Avoid **harmful sexual activity**.
- Avoid **telling lies**.
- Avoid **alcohol** and **drugs**.

## Right Livelihood

Buddhists must choose a career carefully if they are to follow the Five Precepts.

- **Applying** the **Five Precepts** in **business**.
- Jobs to be avoided might include: the army, working in a pub, working as a butcher.

## Environment

- Care for the environment is due to **loving kindness** to all **creatures**.
- Buddhists should try **not** to **damage the earth**.
- As everything is **dependent on everything else** we are not superior to anything else.
- Buddhists remind us that the **world** is **not just** there **for humans**.
- This is why **humans** a have a **duty to care** for the **environment**.
- The aim should be to enable all things to **live** in **harmony**.
- Some (monks) choose to be **vegetarians** out of **respect for life**.

# 8.10 Scriptures

Buddhists have many forms of **scripture**, some of which are regarded as more important than others. Make sure you understand which texts are found in which '**basket**'.

- The **earliest scriptures** are called **Tripitaka** or **Three Baskets**.
- The **first basket** has **rules** for **monks** and **nuns**.
- The **second basket** has the **teachings** of the **Buddha**.
- Second basket also contains the **Dhammapada** and is the most **popular Buddhist scripture**.
- Second basket also contains the **Jataka Tales**. These are **stories** of the **former lives** of the **Buddha**.
- The **third basket** is Buddhist **philosophical teaching**.
- **Zen Buddhists do not have scriptures** but rely on the teachings of **teachers handed down**.
- **Japanese** Buddhists use **koans** which are **short questions** or **sayings**.
- One **famous** koan is, '**what is the sound of one hand clapping?**'.

# Summary

You should now know the following:

1. The role of Siddhartha.
2. The main teachings of the Dharma.
3. The importance of Sangha.
4. The various types of Buddhism.
5. The meaning of 'taking refuge'.
6. The various types of Buddha images.
7. The use of a shrine or temple.
8. The various Buddhist festivals.
9. How Buddhists live their lives.
10. The different Buddhist scriptures.

# Test yourself

Before moving on to the next chapter, make sure you can answer the following questions. The answers are on pages 185-186.

1.  Describe Siddhartha's (the Buddha) quest and the four sights. (5)

2.  Explain what is meant by the sangha. (5)

3.  Describe briefly any **two** different kinds of Buddhism. (5)

4.  Explain Buddhists' use of images in worship. (5)

5.  Describe the main teachings on the Buddhist way of life. (5)

# Chapter 9: World religions: Sikhism

You only need to revise a minimum of one world religion for the examination. If you are not sure which one to revise, then check with your teacher.

---

**BCE** means **Before the Common Era** and is equivalent to using bc.

**CE** means the **Common Era** and is equivalent to using AD.

---

These revision notes follow the order of Philip Emmett's *The Sikh Experience*. You must make sure that you understand and learn the ideas in *The Sikh Experience* as well as the notes below.

Use the ideas in *Study Skills* by Elizabeth Holtom, published by Galore Park, to help you remember these notes and ideas.

The **Ten Gurus**, or **teachers**, formed Sikhism in the years 1469–1708 CE. You will need to know the following points about the most important Gurus.

## 9.1 Guru Nanak

- **Guru Nanak** was born near **Lahore** in **1469 CE** in **Pakistan**.
- He was the first of the **Ten Gurus** (a **religious teacher**).
- He was the **son** of **high caste Hindu** parents.
- His **intelligence** and **wisdom impressed his teachers** at an early age.
- One story tells how, as a **child**, a **deadly cobra shaded** him from the **sun**.
- On one occasion he used his pocket **money to help the poor**.
- He **married** when he was **16**.
- He became an **accountant** for a **Muslim leader**.
- He was well **known** for his **honesty**.
- He **prayed** a lot and one day when he came out of a **river** he felt the strong **presence of God**.
- **Three days later** he set out to **teach** people how to **pray**, **live pure lives** and **give generously**.
- He went on **four great teaching journeys** accompanied by his **friend** and musician **Mardana**.
- In **1521 CE** he **founded** a new town, **Kartarpur**, as the **first Sikh community**.
- The first **free kitchen** or **langar** was founded. Free meals were served to visitors.

- He **died** in **1539 CE**.
- He appointed **Lehna** to be his **successor**.

## 9.2 The Gurus after Guru Nanak

The text book (*The Sikh Experience*) mentions the following gurus but you do not need to know about them for the examination: Guru Amar Das, Guru Ram Das, Guru Arjan Dev, Guru Hargobind, Guru Har Rai, Guru Har Krishnan, Guru Tegh Bahadur.

## 9.3 Guru Angad

- **Angad** was **appointed** to be guru just **before Guru Nanak died**.
- Called **Lehna** but **renamed Angad**, which means 'part of my body'.
- He was a man of **humility**, **devotion** and **commitment**.
- He **taught** people that **salvation** is achieved through **performing their duties**.
- He taught his **disciples** to be **physically fit**.
- He **collected** together **Guru Nanak's hymns**.
- These hymns are **collected** in the **Guru Granth Sahib**.
- He **developed** the **free kitchen**.

## 9.4 Guru Gobind Rai

- He was the **last** of the **Ten Gurus**.
- He was **later called Guru Gobind Singh**.
- He was a **strong leader** and **challenged** the **emperor**.
- He restored the Sikh's faith in God.
- He **trained Sikhs** to be **soldiers** to protect the rights and beliefs of others.
- He wrote **poetry** to give **spiritual strength**.
- The **Sikhs** grew in **confidence** under his leadership.

## 9.5 Vaisakhi 1699 CE

- A large number of **Sikhs** had **met** to **celebrate Vaisakhi** in **1699 CE**.
- **Gobind Rai** asked for **volunteers** who would **give** their **heads** for him.
- **Five volunteers** presented themselves and each time **Gobind Rai appeared** with a **sword dripping** with the **blood** of the volunteer.
- Then the **five men** appeared **unharmed**.

- These five men were the **formation** of the **Panj Pyares** or 'five beloved ones'.

- They became the **basis** of the **Khalsa** or '**pure community**'.

- The five become **members** of the **Khalsa** by eating a **special food** called **Amrit**.

- All members of the **Khalsa** are called **Singh** or lion; **Kaur** or princess.

- Gobind Rai insisted on **high standards of dress**.

- **Gobind Rai** was **murdered** in **1708 CE** by one of his enemies.

- He said in the **future** there would be **no more gurus**.

- The guru would be the **Sikh scriptures**, or the **Guru Granth Sahib**.

## 9.6 The Khalsa

The most dedicated Sikhs form the Khalsa, a body of followers who live with the highest moral standards.

- The **Khalsa** are **those** who are **willing to die for** the **Guru** and **Sikhism**.

- **Not all Sikhs** are members of the **Khalsa**.

- **Khalsa** members adopt the **new name** of **Singh** or **Kaur**.

- They have to **live** to **high moral standards**.

- **Singh** means **lion** and describes how **men** are to be strong, caring, and fearless.

- **Kaur** means **princess** and describes how **women** should be treated like a princess.

- Men and women members of the Khalsa **wear five symbols**, the 'The Five Ks'.

### The five Ks are

- **Kesh – uncut hair**, a sign of saintliness as it is a gift from God.

- **Kangha – comb**, keeps uncut hair tidy. Men wear turbans.

- **Kara – steel band** on right hand. It is a sign that **God is eternal**. It is also a sign of the **unity** and strength of the Khalsa.

- **Kachha – shorts** (underclothes) are a sign of **duty** to others and action.

- **Kirpan – sword**, a sign of **freedom** and a duty to **protect the weak**.

## 9.7 Guru Granth Sahib

On his death in 1708 CE, **Guru Gobind Rai** said that there would be no more gurus in human form. Instead Sikhs regard a **religious text**, the **Guru Granth Sahib**, as the **final** and **eternal guru**.

- **Guru** means **religious teacher**.

- The role of the guru is to **lead** people from **darkness into light**.

- There were **no more human gurus after the death of the tenth Guru Gobind Singh**.

- The role of the guru was **carried on** by the **Sikh scriptures** – the **Guru Granth Sahib**.

- The **scriptures** include the **teachings** of the **first five gurus**.

- They were **first compiled** by **Guru Arjan**.

- It contains many **hymns** arranged according to their **tunes** or **ragas**.

- It is written in the **Gurmukhi script**.

- It is **respected** but **not worshipped**.

- It is considered to be the **Word of God**.

- Given the **place of honour** in the **Gurdwara**.

- It must be **present** at all **important ceremonies**.

- When **moved** at a ceremony it **must be carried on a person's head**.

- It must be **wrapped in clean decorated cloths**.

- Many have a separate room at **home** called a **gurdwara** to read the **Guru Granth Sahib**.

- Its teachings are called **gurbani**.

- Many **homes** keep and read a **shortened version** called the **Gutka**.

## 9.8 Rahit Maryada

Sikhs must base their everyday lives on a special **code of conduct** called the **Rahit Maryada**.

- **Rahit** means **discipline**.

- In the **first Khalsa** Guru Gobind Singh laid down clear rules.

- Over time some **new rules** were added, which caused **dispute**.

- In **1945 the rules** were **made clear** in the **Rahit Maryada**.

- It has been **translated** into **English**.

- It explains that a **Sikh** is anyone who believes in **one God**, the **Ten Gurus'** teaching, the **Guru Granth Sahib**, **baptism** by **Amrit** and is **not a member of another religion**.

- It expects **Sikhs** to **meet together** and **think** about **gurbani**, the teaching of the Guru Granth Sahib.

### The Rahit's teaching on Sikh family life

- A Sikh must **pray to God** before carrying out any task.
- **Children** must be **educated**.
- **Children's hair** should **not be cut**.
- **No Sikh** should take any **drug, alcohol, tobacco**.
- **Women** may **not pierce their bodies** for jewellery.
- **Women** may **not wear** a **face veil**.

### The Rahit's teaching on life in the community

- Every Sikh must give **money to help the poor**.
- There must be **no gambling**.
- Sikhs should **never steal**.
- Every Sikh should aim to be involved with **voluntary work**.

## 9.9 Beliefs

### God

- Beliefs about God are found in the **Mul Mantra prayer** written by **Guru Nanak**.
- God is **Truth**.
- There is **only one** God.
- God is the **beginning and end** of everything.
- God is the **designer** and **creator**.
- God is **timeless**.
- God is **self-existent** (he does not depend on anything else for his existence).
- God's **Name** is most important and should be remembered and **repeated** by Sikhs.
- God's name is remembered by reciting the **Waheguru** or **Wonderful Lord**.

### Reincarnation

- **Reincarnation** is the **rebirth** and refers to those who have been **selfish and ignored God's will**.
- Rebirth is caused by being **envious** of others or greed.
- **Mukti** means **release from rebirth**.

- **Mukti** is **given by God's grace**.
- **Release** comes by **listening** to the **gurbani**.
- Release also comes by listening and **meditating** on the **Name of God**.

## Gurus

- A **guru** is a **religious leader**.
- It is important for a Sikh to have a good **upright person** as their guru.
- He **leads** people from **dark to light**.
- The guru **teaches** people **about the Guru Granth Sahib**.
- The Guru Granth Sahib contains the teaching of human Gurus about God's Will.

# 9.10 Birth and initiation

## Birth

- **The mother** and **family attend** the **gurdwara**.
- **The parents** bring the new **baby** to the **front** of the **gurdwara**.
- The **baby is held above** the **Guru Granth Sahib**.
- Special **thanksgiving hymns** are sung.
- The **Guru Granth Sahib** is **opened** at **random**.
- The **name** of the child must start with the **first letter** of the **hymn on that page**.
- Sometimes a **kirpan** (sword) is dipped in **amrit** (honey and water) and **touched** on the **baby's tongue**.
- The **Ardas** prayer is said.
- The special **Karah Parshad** food is distributed.

## Amritsanskar or initiation

Initiation occurs around the age of 15. The people wishing to become Khalsa Sikhs must show themselves willing to follow the Sikh way of life and wear the Five Ks.

- Attended by **five Sikhs** who are **full members** of the **Khalsa**.
- They **wear** the **Five Ks** and **special saffron coloured robes**.
- It takes place **privately** in the **gurdwara**.
- The ceremony begins with a **reading** from the **Guru Granth Sahib**.
- Those being **initiated** are asked **various questions**.

- Questions include: 'Do you believe in **one God?**' and 'Will you live by **Sikh teachings?**'.

- **Amrit** is prepared by the **five amrit-dhari** Sikhs with a double-edged **sword**.

- The **candidates** receive the **amrit five times**.

- The **Mul Matra** is said **five times**.

- The **rules** of **Khalsa** are **explained**.

- The **Ardas** is said and **a final reading** from the **Guru Granth Sahib**.

- **Some** Sikhs do **not join** the **Khalsa** but **keep** to its **rules**.

- They are called **kesh-dhari**.

## 9.11 Gurdwara

A Sikh **temple** is called a **Gurdwara**, which means **door to the Guru**. The Gurdwara is used for worship, study and many other community activities. A typical gurdwara will be laid out as follows:

- A **saffron flag** or **Nishan Sahib** hangs outside with the symbol of the **Khalsa**.

- Shoes are **taken off** before entering and **head covered**.

- The **main Hall** is called the **diwan** and contains many **pictures** of the **Gurus**.

- The **palki** is a **raised platform** and **canopy**.

- The **Guru Granth Sahib** is placed in the **palki** on a **stool** or **manji**.

- The whole of this **area** is called **takht** or **throne**.

- The **Guru Granth Sahib** is **protected** by a **person waving** a **fan** or **chauri**.

- **Another room** is set aside for the **Guru Granth Sahib** to be kept at **night time**.

- Other rooms are for meetings, library, schoolrooms, etc.

### Worship or diwan in the Gurdwara

- **Worshippers** approach the **takht** and make an **offering**.

- Everyone **sits** on the floor with **crossed legs**.

- **Diwan** consists of **hymns** or **kirtan** sung by the **ragis** (singers).

- Everyone **meditates** on the **Name of God**.

- There may be **talks** on the **teachings** of the **Gurus**.

- The **holy sweet** or **Karah Parshad** is placed **near** the **Guru Granth Sahib**.

- **Karah Parshad** is made from **sugar**, **butter** and **semolina**.

- At the **end** of the service the **Japji** is said.

- Everyone **faces** the **Guru Granth Sahib** for a final **reading**.

- The **final prayer** asks **God to accept** the **Karah Parshad**.

- Everyone is **given** some of the **Karah Parshad**.

## The langar or free kitchen

- The **langar** was first **established** by **Guru Nanak**.

- It makes sure people from **different backgrounds eat together**.

- It is a sign of **equality**.

- The **food** is always the **same** for everyone.

- Those who **prepare** the food learn about **service to others**.

- The food is usually **vegetarian**.

- It is a custom for **families** to **take it in turns** to buy and prepare the food.

# 9.12 Festivals

While there are many Sikh festivals, you are only expected to know the following two:

## Vaisakhi

- **Vaisakhi** is the **most important** festival.

- Remembers the **foundation** of the **Khalsa**.

- It is also the **Sikh New Year**.

- **Unity**, **courage** and **strength** are celebrated.

- Lots of individual and team **games** are played.

## Diwali

- **Diwali** is also celebrated by **Hindus** (but for different reasons).

- It remembers when **Guru Amar Das** told Sikhs to **gather together**.

- It also remembers when **Guru Hargobind** was **released** from **prison**.

- The story tells how the **emperor allowed** all those who held on to **Guru Hargobind's coat** to be **freed** as well.

- **Kirtan** (singing from the Guru Granth Sahib) takes place in the **gurdwara**.

- **Fireworks** and lighting of **lamps** celebrate Guru Hargobind's release.

## 9.13 Marriage and death

### Marriage

Because the Gurus taught that families were particularly important, Sikhs are strongly encouraged to marry. While Sikh marriages are often arranged, the marriage cannot take place unless both bride and groom agree to it.

- At a **betrothal ceremony** the **girl's family** offer a **kirpan** and **sweets** as a sign of **commitment**.

- Before the ceremony **gifts are exchanged** between families.

- It can take place in the **bride's home** or **gurdwara**.

- **Guru Granth Sahib** must be **present**.

- The **bride** and **groom sit facing** the **takht**.

- The **groom** wears a **scarf of red and gold**.

- They are **told** about their **responsibilities**.

- A **blessing** is said for **them** and their **parents**.

- The couple **bow** to the **Guru Granth Sahib** as a sign of **agreement**.

- **Garlands of flowers** are given to them by the **groom's father**.

- The **groom's father** places the **groom's scarf** in the **bride's hands**.

- The **marriage hymn** by **Guru Ram Das** is **read**.

- The couple **circle** round the **Guru Granth Sahib four times**.

- **Flower petals** are **sprinkled** over the **couple**.

- **Sweets** are given to them by the **bride's parents**.

- **Money** is placed in the couple's laps by **guests**.

- Everyone joins in a **meal**.

### Death and funerals

Sikhs regard death as the result of God's will. The funeral is a time for praising God as much as celebrating the life of the deceased.

- If possible the **gurbani** should be **recited whilst** someone is **dying**.

- When someone has **died** the body is **washed** and dressed in **clean clothes**.

- If the person is a **Khalsa Sikh** then the **Five Ks** are worn.

- Last respects are paid by going to a **service** in the **gurdwara**.

- The body is taken to be **cremated**.

- As the body is being taken to the **crematorium hymns are sung** from the Guru Granth Sahib.

- The **Ardas** is said.

- The body is put on the funeral **pyre**.

- **Evening prayer** is recited.

- The **ashes** can be placed in **flowing water** or **buried**.

- **Mourning** can last up to **10 days**.

# 9.14 Places of pilgrimage

Pilgrimage is the act of making a journey to a place that has a special relevance to a religious belief. People who make them are known as **pilgrims**. The places Sikh pilgrims visit might be the site of an important historical event, such as the birthplace of a guru.

## The Five Takhts

- **Takht** means **throne**.

- The **Five Takhts** are **places** with **spiritual authority** where **religious decisions** are made.

- **Guidance** is offered under the **leaders** of the takhts and the **Guru Granth Sahib**.

- The **chief takht** is **Amritsar** the Akal Takht.

- Other takhts are: **Anandpur**, **Nanded**, **Patna** and **Talwandi Sabo**.

## Harimandir, The Golden Temple at Amritsar

- The **Golden Temple** was founded in the **Punjab** in **1589**.

- It has a large **pool for bathing** and a **temple**.

- The **temple** is **highly decorated**.

- **Worshippers** have to **step down** into the temple as a sign of **humility**.

- There is a lot of **black and white marble** and **precious stones**.

- The **walls** have many **writings from scriptures**.

- **Ground floor** contains the **takht**, **palki** and a **rail to guide worshippers** round the Guru Granth Sahib.

- The **Upper floor** is for **reading** of the Guru Granth Sahib.

- There is a **hall of mirrors** to make the place more **beautiful**.

- The **golden dome** gives the temple its **name**.

# Summary

You should now know the following:

1. The key moments in the life of Guru Nanak.

2. The Gurus after Guru Nanak.

3. The key moments in the life of Guru Angad.

4. The key moments in the life of Guru Gobind Rai.

5. What happened at Vaisakhi 1699 CE and its importance for Sikhism.

6. The significance of the Khalsa.

7. The importance and use of the Guru Granth Sahib.

8. The significance and teachings of the Rahit Maryada.

9. The central Sikh beliefs.

10. The key beliefs and practices regarding birth and initiation.

11. The layout and use of the Gurdwara.

12. The various Sikh festivals.

13. The beliefs and practices regarding marriage and death.

14. The various places of Sikh pilgrimage.

# Test yourself

Before moving on to the next chapter, make sure you can answer the following questions. The answers are on pages 186-187.

| | | |
|---|---|---|
| 1. | Outline the life of Guru Gobind Rai and the first Vaisakhi. | (5) |
| 2. | Explain the main teachings of the Rahit Maryada. | (5) |
| 3. | Explain what Sikhs believe about reincarnation. | (5) |
| 4. | Describe a typical Gurdwara. | (5) |
| 5. | Describe the Harimandir (The Golden Temple at Amritsar). | (5) |

# Test yourself answers

*Marks for each question are given in brackets.*

## Chapter 2: Old Testament texts and contemporary issues

### 1. The Second Creation Story

(a) Adam was punished by having to work and Eve was punished by making childbirth painful. (2)

(b) The Garden of Eden was perfect. In it were two trees, the Tree of Knowledge and the Tree of Life. Adam and Eve were not allowed to eat fruit from the Tree of Knowledge. If they did they would be able to know good and evil. In the garden Adam and Eve lived peacefully with the other animals. One of these animals was a serpent. (6)

(c) This story teaches that humans have a duty to look after the natural world. Everything has its special place and God gave us the responsibility of making sure that harmony is maintained. This means making sure that animals are respected and humans don't use their power to damage the natural environment but to look after it. Because humans share in God's love they should love the world as he does. (6)

(d) Some argue that as God gave us free will, then we must be responsible for our actions. For example, if our parents give us some money to spend, then we are free to use it as we wish; but if we buy something which is dangerous or harmful to someone else, then we know that we should take the blame.

On the other hand, some people think that as we are naturally selfish and rebellious, we cannot be totally responsible for our own actions. For example, some people just get very angry for no reason. In the world there are constant wars and people suffer because governments are corrupt. These definitely seem to support the view in the Bible, for instance in the story of Cain and Abel, that we don't seem to have complete control of our desires.

Therefore I agree with the statement. I don't think we are always responsible for our own actions. (6)

### 2. The Ten Commandments

(a) Sinai is the Mountain of God. (2)

(b) Moses was told that we should have no other gods; that we should keep the Sabbath day holy by working six days and resting on the seventh; that we should honour our father and mother; that we should not murder and steal. (6)

(c) First of all, the commandments teach that the Israelites should be an example or a light to the world. This means keeping to a very high standard of moral goodness. For example, the commandments mean that when you make a promise you should keep to it. This is important so that we trust each other. Secondly, they also teach that as our lives are God-given we should respect other people and their property. It is also wrong to murder because life is not ours but is given by God. (6)

(d) Some people think that the purpose of punishment is not to make people suffer but to make them change their attitudes. Being punished means that if you can feel some of the hurt which you have caused someone else to feel, you might then be sorry for what you have done. This is what Jesus wanted people to do when he asked them to repent and change their ways.

On the other hand, others think that reform is not enough. It doesn't really make the victim feel any better and punishment should make someone suffer by having things taken away from them and for them to experience how angry other people are with them. Therefore, if they have done something really bad, such as murder, then they should be killed.

I don't think we should deliberately make a wrong-doer suffer because this would be an eye for an eye and two wrongs don't make a right. (6)

## 3. David and Bathsheba

(a) Temptation is the desire to do something wrong. (2)

(b) King David saw Bathsheba, the wife of Uriah the Hittite, bathing on her roof. David had sex with her and then set about trying to get rid of Uriah so he could marry Bathsheba. First he got Uriah home to report on the war. He thought if he could do this then Uriah would sleep with Bathsheba and then he would think that she was having his child. But Uriah would not leave his men. David tried to get Uriah drunk but eventually he sent him to the front line where he was killed. Now he could marry Bathsheba. (6)

(c) The story doesn't show David in a very good light. First he was driven by lust, not reason. He used his power to have sex with another man's wife. This is adultery and, as David was supposed to be the 'shepherd of his people', this makes him a hypocrite. Then he misuses his power through cunning and lying by trying to get Uriah to think Bathsheba is having his baby. Finally it shows how cruel David is by having Uriah deliberately killed in battle. (6)

(d) Some think that the more power and authority a person has, then the more they should expect to be punished if they misuse their power. This is because power brings lots of privileges – more money, a bigger house, a great social life. As we see in Nathan's parable, the more someone has the more responsible they have to be with it. It is only fair for them to be punished more as they have had greater advantages.

On the other hand, the law should treat everyone the same. For example, whether it is someone like Harold Shipman, who misused his responsibility as a doctor to kill many of his patients, or a thug who kills another person in a fight, they have both killed and both should be treated equally under the law.

However, I agree that it is only fair to punish someone more who has misused their authority because they should know better. (6)

## 4. Amos' message

(a) Justice means treating others fairly. (2)

(b) Amos' message taught that the leaders of Israel were corrupt. He said they were worshipping false idols and exploiting the poor by taking grain from them for no payment. The rich were also bribing the courts so they wouldn't be punished. Even good people are condemned because they have failed to speak out. Amos said God would come and judge Israel and bring justice rolling down like a river. (6)

(c) Amos put his message in very strong terms so that the rich landowners would understand that even though they thought they could get away with exploiting the poor, God would punish them. He hoped they would repent. Repentance means to turn back to God and change your ways. Amos describes justice as a river so that it would cleanse them of their sins. Justice would also mean equality so rich and poor could live together in harmony. (6)

(d) Some argue that as a nation we are very well off and we therefore have a duty to help those people in the world who are much poorer than we are by buying Fair Trade products. This appears to be very reasonable. If we want to make the world a better place then we should learn from Amos' message; if we don't we might find that in the future we are the ones living in poverty.

On the other hand, if we only buy Fair Trade products then our own farmers might find they are losing money and we would also be being disloyal to people in our own country. This could also lead to injustice. Fair Trade products are also a lot more expensive and that could make people who buy them worse off.

I think we should try to use Fair Trade products if we can but we shouldn't be forced to buy *only* their products. (6)

# Chapter 3: New Testament texts and contemporary issues

## 1. On being a follower of Jesus: the rich young man

(a) Sacrifice means giving up something for something else of greater value. (2)

(b) A rich man came up to Jesus and asked him what he should do to inherit eternal life. Jesus told him he should keep the Ten Commandments. The man said he had kept all these since he was a child. Jesus set him a further challenge. He told the man that he should now sell everything and give the money to the poor. The man went away very sad because he was unable to do this. (6)

(c) In Jesus' time having great wealth was a sign that a person had been blessed by God. So the man's question to Jesus was really asking Jesus to confirm that he was a good person. He wants Jesus to praise him. But Jesus' challenge is to test whether the man really understands what justice means and to reverse the usual ideas in society and look after the weak and the poor. Looking after the poor is a sign of true discipleship. But the rich man cannot be a disciple because he is thinking only about himself. (6)

(d) Having great wealth is not good because it often means a person is more interested in getting money than being really concerned for others. That is why Jesus said that it was easier for a camel to pass through the eye of a needle than for a rich man to enter the Kingdom of God. Mother Teresa is a good example of someone who dedicated her life to the poor because she knew that this would bring her greater happiness than being very rich.

On the other hand, having great wealth is a chance to use money wisely for others. If there weren't rich people in the world there would be nobody to give money to people like Mother Teresa who worked to help the poor.

I think that people should have wealth but I don't think *great* wealth is good because it doesn't usually make people happy. (6)

## 2. Who was Jesus? Peter's declaration

(a) Son of Man refers to Jesus' role as the one who would suffer for others. (2)

(b) On the road to Caesarea Philippi Jesus asked the disciples who the people they were preaching to thought he was. They answered that some thought he was John the Baptist, some thought he was Elijah or a prophet. Jesus then asked his disciples who they thought he was. Peter answered that Jesus was the messiah. Then Jesus told them that the Son of Man would suffer many things and then be killed. (6)

(c) When Jesus explained that he would suffer as a messiah, he probably knew that this wasn't what the disciples thought the messiah should be. They all imagined that the messiah would bring a time of peace, compassion and justice. Jesus' healings and treatment of the outcasts show that this is true. But Peter's words show that he cannot understand how Jesus' suffering will achieve these things. Jesus' idea is that the messiah must suffer for others. (6)

(d) Some might argue that Jesus must have been more than a good man because good people don't usually have power to cure the sick and even bring people back to life again, as he did to Jairus's daughter. That is why for Christians he is the Son of God. His resurrection is proof of this.

On the other hand there is no proof that the resurrection took place and it may just be a story to explain how Jesus' message inspired his disciples after his death. But Jesus did do a lot of good and he challenged people to be loving and kind to each other.

I agree that Jesus was no more than a good man because it is difficult to know what the resurrection means, but his life is a very good example of someone who was prepared to die for what he believed in. (6)

## 3. Parables: The Sower

(a) A parable is a story or saying comparing the Kingdom of God with everyday human events. (2)

(b) A sower went out to sow the seed on his field. Some seed fell on the path and was eaten by birds. Some seed fell on rocky ground and grew for a while and then died for lack of moisture. Some fell amongst the thorns and grew but then was choked by them. Some fell on good ground and produced a hundred per cent more than was sown. (6)

(c) Jesus told parables to explain in everyday terms his teaching about the Kingdom of God. The Kingdom of God is about God's special relationship with us. This parable is about how different people react to Jesus' teaching about the Kingdom. Some reject it without ever listening to it. Others listen for a while but don't make a real effort to meet its challenge and others like the idea but prefer their money and wealth. The parable is to encourage the disciples to keep going, because many will listen and the spiritual rewards are great. (6)

(d) This is a very sweeping statement but it is true that many people don't really think deeply about what they believe is important. Some are happy just to get on with life doing the shopping, going to the football match, watching TV and having a good time, just as Jesus taught in the parable of the sower. Not a huge number of people go to church and many people aren't interested in politics because they don't vote.

On the other hand most of the population say they believe in God and more people in the world belong to a religion than those who do not. When people die or there is suffering in the family, then people often express their beliefs clearly.

I think all people have beliefs but as these are often quite private it is difficult to know whether they hold them strongly or not. (6)

## 4. The early Christians: how the early Christians lived

(a) Worship is giving God praise and honour. (2)

(b) The early Christians met in small groups and worshipped together. They studied the teachings of the Apostles and worshipped by breaking bread and praying. They shared everything they had. Those who had property sold it and gave it to the poor. Those in Jerusalem worshipped every day in the Temple. (6)

(c) The early Christians believed that although Jesus had died on the cross, he had been resurrected. They believed the Holy Spirit was with them. This is why they worshipped frequently together and shared bread to remember how Jesus often shared his meals with them and especially his last supper. They also followed Jesus' teaching about helping the poor and needy. They had quite radical beliefs about equality and practised communism. (6)

(d) Jesus taught that we should love our neighbour and that means that Christians shouldn't disagree with each other. Jesus told off James and John for causing discontent amongst the disciples by wanting to have the best places in the Kingdom of God. Of course there may be minor disagreements but the point of Christianity is to respect everyone and so it would be hypocritical if Christians didn't get on with each other.

On the other hand, disagreement can be good. Often Jesus taught in a way which made people disagree and this helped them to understand his teaching. Disagreement shows that Christianity has some very difficult ideas which need different explanations. For example, Peter and Judas both had different ideas of the kind of messiah Jesus should be.

I think Christians should be allowed to disagree with each other, but it is not right for one group to think it is better than another one because Jesus taught that his followers should respect each other. (6)

# Chapter 4: World Religions

## Chapter 4: Christianity

1. Jesus was born in Bethlehem to Mary and Joseph. We don't know much about his early life but when he was 30 he was baptised by John the Baptist and started to preach in Galilee. His teaching upset the leaders of Judaism. His disciple Judas betrayed him to the Jewish authorities who handed him over to the Romans. Pilate had Jesus crucified. But three days later Jesus rose from the dead and later ascended to heaven. (5)

2. Most Christians marry in a church. The service begins when the minister explains the purpose of marriage and then the bride and bridegroom make their promises to each other. They promise to love, honour and protect each other for the rest of their lives. Then they may exchange rings and the minister says they have now become husband and wife. (5)

3. The Bible is important for Christians because they believe it to be the Word of God. That means it is not like any other book but was inspired by the Holy Spirit and can therefore guide Christians in their daily lives. Many Christians study the Bible in groups or listen to it being read in church as part of their worship of God. (5)

4. Christians believe that there is only one God who created everything. But they also believe that he exists as the Trinity. As Father he creates everything, as Son he becomes human in the person of Jesus Christ and as Holy Spirit he is everywhere. It is as the Holy Spirit that God is able to be a source of inspiration for Christians today. (5)

5. Christians often go on pilgrimage to the Holy Land (modern Israel). They may visit Bethlehem where Jesus was born and go to the Church of the Nativity. Some travel to Galilee where Jesus spent most of his life and to Capernaum where he taught. Most importantly pilgrims go to Jerusalem and follow the road which Jesus took on his way to his crucifixion. This road is called the Via Dolorosa. (5)

## Chapter 5: Judaism

1. For Orthodox Jews a body should be buried as soon after a person has died as possible. The body is prepared and dressed in a white garment. After the body is buried everyone washes their hands in a special ceremony. It is usual for the bereaved family to stay at home for a week and for people to visit them. Men do not shave and women do not wear make up. The kaddish prayer is said in the synagogue. (5)

2. The Shabbat begins at sunset when the mother of the family lights two candles and says a special blessing. During the day she will have prepared the house and her husband and boys may have attended the synagogue. When he returns the father says kiddush over the wine and a blessing over the special Hallah bread. After eating the bread and wine the family eat the Shabbat meal and at the end sing Jewish songs. (5)

3. The Torah consists of the first five books of the Tenach and contains the 613 commandants needed for Jews to live good lives. Jews also believe that Moses was given the Oral Torah, which is all the other laws and teachings needed to keep the written Torah. This is called the Talmud. Talmud means to study. (5)

4. Jews believe in two ages – the present age and the coming of a world where there will be no violence, where everyone will live in peace with one another and there will be justice for everyone forever. They believe that the messiah will come first and prepare the world for its coming. Some believe that the World to Come could be the after-life in heaven. (5)

5. Sukkot is an Autumn festival which commemorates the time when the Israelites were wandering in the wilderness and living in tents. Today Jews build a tent or sukkah and decorate it with fruits. If it is warm enough they live in it during the eight days of the festival. At the synagogue service people hold bundles of willow, palm and myrtle and carry a citron fruit which is waved in the four directions of the world. (5)

## Chapter 6: Islam

1. Muhammad had been meditating in a cave on Mount Hira outside Makkah when suddenly the angel Gabriel appeared and told him to read. Muhammad said he couldn't read but the angel squeezed him. This happened two more times and on the third time Muhammad was able to recite God's words. This left him greatly shocked but he was encouraged by his wife Khadijah to believe that it was God who had spoken to him. (5)

2. Muslims believe that the Qur'an is God's final revelation to the world given directly to Muhammad over a period of twenty-three years. It cannot really be translated and should be read in Arabic. Many people learn it by heart. The Hadith are various books which contain the words and actions of Muhammad and are consulted to see how Muhammad understood the Qur'an. (5)

3. Muslims believe that angels are God's messengers. They cannot usually be seen and are made of light. They can take on human form, just as Gabriel did when he brought the Qur'an to Muhammad. Everyone has at least one guardian angel who looks after you when you pray. They can be felt as a presence of love and peace. (5)

4. When a Muslim arrives in Makkah he changes into simple white clothes to prepare himself for spiritual purity or ihram. There are lots of ceremonies to carry out. The important ones are circling the Ka'bah seven times and running between the two hills and the Zamzam well. After camping he stands in the Plain of Arafat and prays to God. Then he throws stones at the pillars of Mina to drive out Satan before returning to Makkah. (5)

5. It is expected in Islam that men and women will marry. Sex should only occur within marriage. They should both dress modestly and set a good example to their children. This means that husbands and wives should respect their parents and educate and feed their children as best as they can. Husbands must provide money for the family and protect their wives. Wives must look after their guests and feed the hungry. (5)

## Chapter 7: Hinduism

1. The story is about the battle between good and evil and is told as a war between two warring families. The blind eldest Kuru brother couldn't become king so he let his brother Pandu rule instead. But Pandu wanted to become a holy man so he gave the kingdom to his brother Dhritavashtra. But Dhritavashtra's sons tried to kill Pandu's sons. Pandu's sons escaped, led by Arjuna. In a great battle the Pandus defeated the Kurus and ruled wisely afterwards. (5)

2. Atman means soul. Every living thing has atman and when it dies the atman leaves the body and moves on to another body. This is called samsara. Samsara also describes the process of change we all go through in our lives. For example, my character is not the same now as when I was little, but I am deep down the same person. Atman is also part of Brahman. (5)

3. The festival of Holi takes place at spring. It remembers the time when the wicked Princess Holika tried to kill her nephew but was burned in the fire instead. So at the festival bonfires are lit. As the festival also remembers Lord Krishna, who liked practical jokes, this is also a time of playing lots of tricks on people. Children are allowed to be cheeky to adults. (5)

4. After the bride has prepared herself and put on her best sari the wedding begins when the couple take seven steps round a fire. This symbolises their hope for children and happiness in the presence of God. They also carry a scarf to show how their lives are now joined together. On the final step they are now husband and wife. Sometimes rice grain is sprinkled over the couple. (5)

5. Worship in the temple begins when a person enters the building and rings a bell to tell the deity he has arrived. Some people sing hymns or prayers. The priest performs arti by passing around a lamp and the people place their hands near it to come into the presence of God. Worshippers make offerings to the deity of money, food and flowers and in return the priest gives them prashad or special food. (5)

## Chapter 8: Buddhism

1. Siddartha set out from his palace because he wanted to see what the real world was like. He saw an old person, then a sick person, then a dead person and finally a holy man. This showed him that the world is full of decay and suffering. But the holy man taught him that a life of prayer and meditation might help him to live a contented life. That was what he set off to find. (5)

2. The sangha is the worldwide community of all Buddhists. However, it often refers to Buddhist monks and nuns who have special duties. In the sangha all people are equal but the duty of a monk is to study the Buddha's Dharma and to live in a vihara or monastery. Monks and nuns have a duty to teach Dharma so they can achieve enlightenment. (5)

3. Zen Buddhism teaches that everyone has a Buddha nature. People can discover their Buddha nature through careful training of the mind and becoming aware of all their actions. This is why flower arranging or tea ceremonies are important.

   In Tibetan Buddhism meditation is important and it is done through special chants or mantras. The Tibetan monks like debates. At festivals there is a lot of dancing and music. (5)

4. The images are used to help in meditation. Some images of the Buddha show various moments in his life and are useful to explain how he learnt to live by the middle way. Other images express some of the inner experiences of the Buddha. Some images are of bodhisattvas, or other beings who have become enlightened. All these images can be used in a shrine at home. (5)

5. The main teaching is found in the Five Precepts. These teach that Buddhists should avoid killing deliberately and not take things which do not belong to them. They should not tell lies or do anything which causes harm to others. They should earn their money fairly and avoid working in jobs such as the army which involves killing people. They should treat the environment with loving kindness.(5)

## Chapter 9: Sikhism

1. Guru Gobind Rai was the last of the Ten Gurus. He was a strong leader and managed to restore the Sikh faith in God. He was famous for training Sikhs to become soldiers and to protect the weak. In 1699 at Vaisakhi, Gobind Rai asked for volunteers to give their heads for him. Five did, but Gobind Rai didn't actually kill them – it was a test of their dedication. This group became the basis of the Khalsa or pure community. (5)

2. The Rahit Maryada is a book setting out how a Sikh should live his life. It teaches that a Sikh is anyone who believes in the one God, the teaching of the ten Gurus and baptism by Amrit. It teaches that in the family children must be educated and their hair should not be cut. It teaches that no Sikh should drink alcohol or take drugs. It also teaches that Sikhs should do voluntary work in the community. (5)

3. Sikhs believe that if you have not lived an entirely good life and have been selfish and ignored God's will then you will be reborn to live another life. If however you have listened to the gurbani and meditated on God's Name and not been envious of others or greedy, then you receive mukti. Mukti is to be released by God from the cycle of rebirths. (5)

4. Gurdwaras usually have a saffron flag flying outside the temple with the sign of the Khalsa on it. In the main hall or diwan of the temple there are pictures of the great Gurus. On the palki the Guru Granth Sahib is placed on a stool or manji. Over the palki is a canopy. There is another room for the Guru Granth Sahib to be kept over night. Other rooms are for teaching and preparation of food. (5)

5. One of the great sights of the Golden Temple is its large pool for bathing and the golden dome. The temple itself is beautifully decorated with black and white marble and many precious stones. The walls are covered by passages from the Sikh scriptures and there is a hall of mirrors. On the ground floor are the takht and the palki. There is a room upstairs for reading the Guru Granth Sahib. (5)

# Appendix

This is how a typical examination paper is laid out. (Please refer to page 1 for details of how the exam instructions will be changing from September 2008.)

## SECTION 1: OLD TESTAMENT TEXTS AND CONTEMPORARY ISSUES

Answer **one** of the following.

1. **The Second Creation Story**

   (a) Name two ways God punished Adam and Eve. (2)

   (b) Describe the main features of the Garden of Eden. (6)

   (c) Explain what the creation story teaches about human stewardship of the world. (6)

   (d) 'We are not always responsible for the consequences of our actions.' Do you agree? Give reasons to support your answer. (6)

2. **The Ten Commandments**

   (a) What is Sinai? (2)

   (b) Describe any five of the Ten Commandments. (6)

   (c) Explain what this story teaches about the relationship between God and humans. (6)

   (d) 'The aim of any punishment is to make the wrong-doer suffer.' Do you agree? Give reasons to support your answer. (6)

3. **David and Bathesheba**

   (a) What is temptation? (2)

   (b) Describe how David came to marry to Bathsheba. (6)

   (c) Explain what this story teaches about David as a ruler. (6)

   (d) 'Leaders should be punished more if they misuse their authority.' Do you agree? Give reasons to support your answer. (6)

4. **Amos' message**

   (a) What is meant by justice? (2)

   (b) Describe Amos' message of judgement on Israel. (6)

   (c) Explain Amos' teaching on justice and repentance. (6)

   (d) 'We should only buy Fair Trade products.' Do you agree? Give reasons to support your answer. (6)

(Total marks for this section: 20)

## SECTION 2: NEW TESTAMENT TEXTS AND CONTEMPORARY ISSUES

Answer **one** of the following.

1. **On being a follower of Jesus: the rich young man**

   (a) What does sacrifice mean? (2)

   (b) Outline the story of the Rich Young Man. (6)

   (c) Explain what this story teaches about wealth and discipleship. (6)

   (d) 'No one should have great wealth.' Do you agree? Give reasons to support your answer. (6)

2. **Who was Jesus? Peter's declaration**

   (a) What does the title Son of Man mean? (2)

   (b) Describe the conversation between Jesus and his disciples at Caesarea Philippi. (6)

   (c) Explain what this event teaches about Jesus' role as the Messiah. (6)

   (d) 'Jesus was no more than just a good man.' Do you agree? Give reasons to support your answer. (6)

3. **Parables: The Sower**

   (a) What is the meaning of the term parable? (2)

   (b) Outline the parable of the Sower. (6)

   (c) Explain why Jesus told this parable. (6)

   (d) 'Most people don't have strong beliefs.' Do you agree? Give reasons to support your answer. (6)

4. **The early Christians: how the early Christians lived**

   (a) What is persecution? (2)

   (b) Describe how the early Christians lived. (6)

   (c) Explain the key beliefs of the early Christians. (6)

   (d) 'Christians should not disagree with each other.' Do you agree? Give reasons to support your answer. (6)

(Total marks for this section: 20)

## SECTION 3: WORLD RELIGIONS

Answer **four** questions from one or more sections.

Do not answer this section if you have submitted coursework.

### A. Christianity

1. Describe the main events of Jesus' life. (5)

2. Describe what happens at a typical Christian wedding ceremony. (5)

3. Explain why the Bible is important for Christians. (5)

4. Explain what Christians believe about God. (5)

5. Describe **one** place where Christians go on pilgrimage. (5)

### B. Judaism

6. Describe what happens at a Jewish funeral. (5)

7. Describe how Shabbat is celebrated at home. (5)

8. Describe what Jews believe about the Torah and the Talmud. (5)

9. Describe what Jews believe about the World to Come. (5)

10. Describe any **one** important Jewish festival. (5)

### C. Islam

11. Describe what happened at Muhammad's call. (5)

12. Describe what Muslims believe about the Qur'an and Hadith. (5)

13. Explain what Muslims believe about angels (5)

14. Describe what happens on Hajj (pilgrimage). (5)

15. Describe the roles of men and women in the Muslim family. (5)

### D. Hinduism

16. Describe the story in the Mahabharata (5)

17. Explain the Hindu teaching on atman and samsara (reincarnation). (5)

18. Describe **one** Hindu festival. (5)

19. Describe what happens at a typical Hindu wedding. (5)

20. Describe worship in a Hindu temple. (5)

### E.  Buddhism

21.  Describe Siddhartha's (the Buddha) quest and the four sights.          (5)

22.  Explain what is meant by the sangha.          (5)

23.  Describe briefly any **two** different kinds of Buddhism.          (5)

24.  Explain Buddhists' use of images in worship.          (5)

25.  Describe the main teachings on the Buddhist way of life.          (5)

### F.  Sikhism

26.  Outline the life of Guru Gobind Rai and the first Vaisakhi.          (5)

27.  Explain the main teachings of the Rahit Maryada.          (5)

28.  Explain what Sikhs believe by reincarnation.          (5)

29.  Describe a typical Gurdwara.          (5)

30.  Describe the Harimandir (The Golden Temple at Amritsar).          (5)

(Total marks for this section: 20)